# How Does the Constitution Secure Rights?

# How Does
# the Constitution
# Secure Rights?

*Robert A. Goldwin*
*and William A. Schambra*
*editors*

American Enterprise Institute for Public Policy Research
Washington and London

This book is the third in a series in AEI's project "A Decade of Study of the Constitution," funded in part by a Bicentennial Challenge Grant from the National Endowment for the Humanities. The first book in this series was *How Democratic Is the Constitution?* and the second book was *How Capitalistic Is the Constitution?* both edited by Robert A. Goldwin and William A. Schambra.

**Library of Congress Cataloging in Publication Data**
Main entry under title:

How does the Constitution secure rights?

  (AEI studies; 380)
  "Third in a series in AEI's project 'A decade of
study of the Constitution' "—T.p. verso.
    1. Civil rights—United States.  2. United States—
Constitutional law—Amendments—1st–10th.  I. Goldwin,
Robert A., 1922–    .  II. Schambra, William A.
III. Series.
KF4749.H68   1985      342.73'085      85–4020
                       347.30285
ISBN 0–8447–3522–1 (alk. paper)
ISBN 0–8447–3521–3 (pbk.: alk. paper)

AEI Studies 380

# Contents

The Editors and the Authors — ix

Foreword  *William J. Baroody, Jr.* — xi

Preface  *Robert A. Goldwin and William A. Schambra* — xiii

1  **How the Constitution Protects Our Rights: A Look at the Seminal Years**  *Robert A. Rutland* — 1

2  **The Constitution and the Bill of Rights**  *Herbert J. Storing* — 15

3  **Two Models of Adjudication**  *Owen M. Fiss* — 36

4  **The Constitution as Bill of Rights**  *Walter Berns* — 50

5  **Subsistence Rights: Shall We Secure These Rights?**  *Henry Shue* — 74

6  **American Constitutionalism and Individual Rights**  *Nathan Tarcov* — 101

# The Editors and the Authors

ROBERT A. GOLDWIN is resident scholar and director of constitutional studies at the American Enterprise Institute. He has served in the White House as special consultant to the president and, concurrently, as adviser to the secretary of defense. He has taught at the University of Chicago and at Kenyon College and was dean of St. John's College in Annapolis. He is the editor of *A Nation of States* and coeditor of *How Democratic Is the Constitution?* and *How Capitalistic Is the Constitution?* He is the author of, most recently, "Three Human Rights Are Enough," *Center Magazine* (July-August 1984).

WILLIAM A. SCHAMBRA is resident fellow at the American Enterprise Institute and was, until recently, the assistant director of constitutional studies at AEI. He is coeditor, with Robert A. Goldwin, of *How Democratic Is the Constitution?* and *How Capitalistic Is the Constitution?* and author of "The Roots of the American Public Philosophy."

WALTER BERNS is John M. Olin Distinguished Scholar in Constitutional and Legal Studies at the American Enterprise Institute and professorial lecturer in constitutional law at Georgetown University. He is the author of *Freedom, Virtue, and the First Amendment, The First Amendment and the Future of American Democracy,* and *For Capital Punishment,* and numerous articles on constitutional issues in professional journals and popular magazines. He has served as professor of political science at Yale, Cornell, and the University of Toronto.

OWEN M. FISS is professor of law at Yale Law School and is the author of *Injunctions, The Civil Rights Injunction, The Structure of Procedure* and "The Forms of Justice" as well as numerous articles in law reviews and professional journals. He served as law clerk for Justices Thurgood Marshall and William J. Brennan and as special assistant, in charge of the Civil Rights Division, to the assistant attorney general of the United States.

ROBERT A. RUTLAND, editor of *The Papers of James Madison* and *The Papers of George Mason*, is professor of history at the University of Virginia. He is author of *The Birth of the Bill of Rights, 1776–1791, The Ordeal of the Constitution, The Newsmongers*, and *The Democrats from Jefferson to Carter*.

HENRY SHUE is senior research associate of the Center for Philosophy and Public Policy at the University of Maryland, College Park. His work on human rights include *Basic Rights: Subsistence, Affluence, and U.S. Foreign Policy* and an article entitled "Torture." He is currently working on a volume dealing with the moral issues surrounding nuclear strategy.

HERBERT J. STORING was, at the time of his death in 1977, the Robert Kent Gooch Professor of Government and director of the Program on the Presidency of the White Burkett Miller Center for Public Affairs, University of Virginia. He was the author of *The Complete Anti-Federalist* and *Black American Political Thought* and the editor of *What Country Have I? Political Writings by Black Americans* and *Essays on the Scientific Study of Politics*.

NATHAN TARCOV is professor of political science and in the College at the University of Chicago. He is also codirector of the John M. Olin Center for Inquiry into the Theory and Practice of Democracy. His writings include *Locke's Education for Liberty*, "Principle and Prudence in Foreign Policy: The Founders' Perspective," and "A 'Non-Lockean' Locke and the Character of Liberalism."

# Foreword

*How Does the Constitution Secure Rights?* addresses a question that could hardly be more timely given the intense interest in protecting human rights throughout a world in which the enjoyment of rights seems less secure than ever. Although the record of the United States in this matter is not perfect, most people would agree that we enjoy security of rights to a degree found in few other places. It is appropriate, therefore, as we try to perpetuate free institutions at home and encourage them abroad, that we turn to the document that chartered our nation and search therein for the methods by which we have actually secured to average U.S. citizens their rights.

This book is the third in a series being published by "A Decade of Study of the Constitution," AEI's project to help prepare the nation for a thoughtful observance of the bicentennial of the Constitution. The first two books were *How Democratic Is the Constitution?* and *How Capitalistic Is the Constitution?*—also edited by Robert A. Goldwin and William A. Schambra. Through such collections of essays —as well as through conferences and television and radio programs— "A Decade of Study" has attempted to raise again the fundamental political issues that appeared at the time of the founding and that have continued to agitate American politics to this day. The controversy that such issues can generate is well illustrated in these forcefully argued essays, written from various points of view. We are proud to publish this volume as a fitting expression of AEI's belief that the competition of ideas is fundamental to a free society.

WILLIAM J. BAROODY, JR.
President
American Enterprise Institute

# Preface

When the American people proclaimed in 1776 the political principles to which the new republic would be dedicated, they put foremost the self-evident truth that all men are equal because they possess "certain unalienable Rights." Governments, they maintained, are instituted "to secure these Rights." This, then, became the purpose of the documents establishing our own government, the Constitution and its subsequent first ten amendments, commonly called the Bill of Rights. The high standards set for the security of rights by those documents became an important measure of our success or failure as a society; by that measure, we have done remarkably well, most Americans would agree, with some notable and unfortunate exceptions.

We Americans tend to judge not only ourselves but other nations as well by those standards. Indeed, when we seek to distinguish our form of free, liberal democracy from totalitarian or authoritarian regimes of the right or left, we frequently point to the protection of human rights here and the absence of protection for, or the suppression of, human rights elsewhere as the central difference. Concern for the protection of human rights has assumed global dimensions. Some of the most influential documents produced by the international organizations of the postwar world are bills or declarations of rights; and in conferences and publications around the world, public officials, journalists, scholars, and concerned citizens debate the nature of such rights and how they may be brought to all nations of the world.

Considering the breadth and intensity of interest in the security of rights, it is ironic and sad that so few peoples in the world enjoy even a minimal level of such security. Perhaps one of the reasons rights are so often affirmed in speech but denied in practice is that one important question is almost never asked: In those societies where rights are adequately protected, how is it done? That is, how are rights actually secured? How do the elements of such societies—the fundamental political principles, the basic political institutions, the social or class structure, and the arrangement of the economy—combine to make the enjoyment of rights a reality for the average citizen? Because the Constitution is the authoritative embodiment of our fundamental principles and the source of so many of our political, legal, economic, and social institutions, we may approach this issue in the United States by asking: How does the Constitution secure rights?

The answer that comes most quickly to the American mind is likely to be that rights are secured here primarily by the Bill of Rights. Ironically, James Madison, Alexander Hamilton, and other principal drafters of the Constitution were initially opposed to the idea of attaching a Bill of Rights to the Constitution. One of the authors in this volume suggests, therefore, that we have the Bill of Rights as the result of a fortuitous circumstance, namely, James Madison's reluctant yielding to public pressure to change his mind.

The belief that rights are most securely protected when they are numerated and defined in carefully prepared lists is reflected today in the controversy over the inclusion of "new" rights—such as the "subsistence rights" championed by one of our authors—alongside the traditional civil and political rights of the constitutional system.

Another likely American response to the question is that rights are protected primarily by a vigilant, powerful, and active judiciary. An author in this volume argues for that view and suggests that the protection of rights may in fact require courts fundamentally to re-structure major institutions within the society, such as schools, prisons, police departments, and mental hospitals.

For a final approach to the task of securing rights, it is necessary to reconsider the arguments made by Madison, Hamilton, and others against the inclusion of a Bill of Rights in the Constitution. Even without the first ten amendments, Hamilton argued in *Federalist* No. 84, "the Constitution is itself, in every rational sense, and to every useful purpose, A BILL OF RIGHTS." Rights would be secured in America, he argued, because the Constitution carefully delineated (and thereby delimited) the powers of the new government, and assigned them to three mutually checking and balancing branches. This arrangement of institutions helped ensure that neither the government as a whole nor any part of it would become so powerful as to be a threat to rights. Hamilton also believed, with Madison, that the secular, com-mercial republic implicit in the new Constitution would stimulate such a proliferation of economic interests and religious sects that no one interest or sect would form a permanent majority within the society. When such a permanent majority forms around a class interest or a zealously held religious or philosophical belief, they argued (and several of the authors in this volume agree), then rights truly are in danger, and no "parchment barrier" list of rights or sitting judge, however vigilant, will be able for long to prevent oppression of individuals and groups in the permanent minority.

However one answers the question posed by this volume, the essays herein should give the reader a sense of the importance of this often neglected aspect of the debate over human rights. If we can understand how, in fact, our constitutional structure serves to protect rights, then we will be able to strengthen the institutions of liberty at home, and we may even be able to help other nations cultivate such institutions. At a time when the gap between the theory and practice of rights in the world seems only to be growing, no understanding could be a more valuable contribution to the safety and happiness of the people of the world.

Robert A. Goldwin
William A. Schambra

# 1

# How the Constitution Protects Our Rights: A Look at the Seminal Years

ROBERT A. RUTLAND

Several biographers of James Madison have taken great pains to fix in our minds the idea that Madison was the "Father of the Constitution." The sick young American nation had at least fifty-five attending physicians when the Federal Convention of 1787 met, but by laying the groundwork for the meeting, by offering a working draft in the Virginia plan, and by his careful efforts to maintain republicanism throughout the convention, Madison surely deserves special praise. If we add to his achievement in Philadelphia his note taking, his authorship of many of *The Federalist* essays, and his role in the Virginia ratifying convention (as well as the whole ratifying process), we must ask, Who has a better claim to be the father of our Constitution? The argument need not detain us long, unless we are devoted Hamiltonians.

Here I argue not for Madison as a constitution maker, but for Madison as the father of our Bill of Rights. In an era not notable for parental respect, I would add that when Madison left Philadelphia in September 1787, he probably would not have liked being called the father of anything—let alone the document he had just signed. Yet so powerful was the weight of public opinion, and so strong the current of Madison's will to save the struggling republic, that two years after Madison had helped bury a bill of rights in Philadelphia, he resurrected it and forced a reluctant Congress to swallow it.

Madison made a mistake at the Federal Convention: he had not cultivated his friendship with George Mason, a fellow delegate from Virginia, but allowed the older man to feel increasingly isolated in the last stages of the convention. On September 12 Mason appealed to the delegates to graft a bill of rights onto the Constitution. Mason said he wished "the plan had been prefaced with a Bill of Rights, and

1

would second a Motion if made for the purpose—It would give great quiet to the people; and with the aid of the State declarations, a bill might be prepared in a few hours."[1] The impatient delegates quickly disposed of Mason's idea by rejecting the plea—unanimously. No doubt Madison was on the winning side, for even the Virginia delegation voted no.

## Public Opinion Favored Bill of Rights

This tactical error had almost immediate repercussions. Mason left the convention in a huff and wrote a brief critique of the Constitution that began: "There is no Declaration of Rights, and the laws of the general government being paramount to the laws and constitution of the several States, the Declarations of Rights in the separate States are no security." This sentence from Mason's pen reverberated throughout the Republic like a thunderclap, forcing friends of the Constitution to seek a series of shelters from the storm of public opinion thus loosed. But as the Federalists of 1788 soon realized, a groundswell of public opinion represents a great deal more than opportunism or rhetoric. Mason's thunderous opening statement touched the people emotionally and forced the supporters of the Constitution to acknowledge that they had erred. An exasperated Federalist in North Carolina complained that the opposition leaders "blow up an idle Fandango about Bills of Rights & Amendments, & what is still more infamous, [threaten to] throw us altogether out of the Union." The echoes of such attacks soon reached Madison.

James Madison lost only one election in his lifetime, and that was owing to his failure to take public opinion into account. When he ran for the Virginia legislature in 1777, he refused to bring a barrel of ardent spirits to the polling place, hoping "to promote, by his example, the proper reform."[2] Public opinion in Orange County, Virginia, held that any man who wanted a freeholder's vote ought to show his appreciation, not his parsimony. Never again did Madison ignore public opinion. Indeed, he spent much of the rest of his life trying either to control it or to understand it. He had been a youngster when public opinion, fanned to ember heat in the Stamp Act controversy, made things uncomfortably warm for Parliament and

---

[1] Max Farrand, ed., *The Records of the Federal Convention of 1787*, 4 vols. (New Haven, Conn.: Yale University Press, 1911, 1937), vol. 2, pp. 587–88.

[2] James Madison, *The Papers of James Madison*, ed. William T. Hutchinson et al., 13 vols. to date (Chicago and Charlottesville: University of Chicago Press, 1962–), vol. 1, p. 193.

Parliament backed off. Public opinion had forced Virginians to make common cause with the people of Massachusetts after the punitive Boston Port Bill reached across the Atlantic. Washington's prestige had carried the convention along despite enormous handicaps; but once back in his home county, Madison realized that he must support a bill of rights to win election to the House of Representatives. He redeemed his campaign pledge by offering a bill of rights at the first session of the new federal Congress. Public opinion? No one knew its might more than Madison, unless it was his neighbor and colleague Thomas Jefferson. "The great extent of our Republic is new," Jefferson said. "Its sparse habitation is new. The mighty wave of public opinion which has rolled over it is new."[3]

## Prodded by Baptist Constituents

Jefferson exulted in this wave because he was riding it as he wrote. Surely Madison respected the political instincts of his old friend Jefferson, who had warned in 1787 that a bill of rights was "what the people are entitled to against every government on earth, general or particular, and what no just government should refuse or rest on inference."[4] Madison's rebuttal was weak. Faced with the complaints of his Baptist friends, who feared persecution for their religious beliefs, he journeyed to Richmond and, when the subject of a bill of rights came up, resorted to argument of *Federalist* No. 10:

> If there were a majority of one sect, a bill of rights would be a poor protection for liberty. Happily for the states, they enjoy the utmost freedom of religion. This freedom arises from that multiplicity of sects, which pervades America, and which is the best and only security for religious liberty in any society. For where there is such a variety of sects, there cannot be a majority of any one sect to persecute the rest.[5]

As Madison saw, the attempt to disregard criticism of the Constitution on the bill of rights issue was not persuasive. A concession, the so-called recommendatory bill of rights offered at the Massachusetts convention, became an urgent issue by the summer of 1788. As John Marshall himself later conceded, "In compliance with a sentiment thus generally expressed, to quiet fears thus extensively entertained,

---

[3] Adrienne Koch and William Peden, eds., *The Life and Selected Writings of Thomas Jefferson* (New York: Random House, 1944), pp. 562–63.

[4] Madison, *Papers*, vol. 10, p. 337.

[5] Ibid., vol. 11, p. 130.

amendments were proposed by the required majority in congress, and adopted by the states."[6]

Madison the father of the Constitution became the father of the Bill of Rights when he realized that his own role in implementing the Constitution was imperiled by hostile public opinion. While running for a House seat, Madison was informed that he had been labeled as hostile to a bill of rights. He went to a great deal of trouble to broadcast a public letter in which he acknowledged his error. The Constitution had been ratified, and circumstances had changed. In his campaign letter Madison said a bill of rights

> in a proper mode, will be not only safe, but may serve the double purpose of satisfying the minds of well meaning opponents, and of providing additional guards in favour of liberty. Under this change of circumstances, it is my sincere opinion that the Constitution ought to be revised, and that the first Congress meeting under it, ought to prepare and recommend to the States for ratification, the most satisfactory provisions for all essential rights, particularly the rights of Conscience in the fullest latitude, the freedom of the press, trials by jury, security against general warrants &c.[7]

Now there was no talk about the freedom guaranteed by any "multiplicity of sects." The people had spoken; Madison listened and made his pledge.

Thus it was that at a most critical stage in our nation's history public opinion forced some able politicians to revise their views about what Madison once called our "parchment barriers." Their decision to drop opposition and add a bill of rights to our Constitution was one of the earliest indications that public opinion cannot be ignored in this country. Alexander Hamilton, who was so often wrong, had tried to tame the dissidents by saying that a bill of rights "would sound much better in a treatise of ethics than in a constitution of government."[8] The other great lawyer at the federal convention, James Wilson, echoing Hamilton's views, said that a bill of rights "was not only unnecessary, but on this occasion it was found impracticable—for who will be bold enough to undertake to enumerate all the rights of the people?"[9] Hamilton and Wilson misread the people's attachment to explicit written statements of their rights;

---

[6] Barron v. Baltimore, 7 Peters 249 (1833).

[7] Madison, *Papers*, vol. 11, pp. 404–5.

[8] *Federalist* No. 84.

[9] Farrand, *Records of the Federal Convention*, vol. 3, p. 143.

Madison knew better after he listened to his neighbors and talked to the Orange County Baptists.

But the role of public opinion in producing the Bill of Rights is not the whole story. The remarkable element in our national and state bills of rights is their effect on public opinion. Research has long since proved that the Revolutionary generation, growing to adulthood in a climate of opinion that fostered freedom of expression, accepted religious toleration as a fundamental tenet of national life. Of course, one was free to criticize Lord North but not so free to defend him; and it was all right to be a Catholic in Boston or a Presbyterian in Maryland in 1776 but better not to make a big point of it. In short, the freedoms our Founding Fathers experienced were relative to the times and places, just as they often are today. Printers who praised George III were few once the Sons of Liberty began to monitor newspapers in Boston and New York. The claim that Samuel Adams single-handedly fomented a revolution is bold but without foundation when we consider the times—the experience of the Boston citizens led them to fan Adams's fiery rhetoric rather than smother it. A tidal wave of public opinion supported the yeomen gathered at Lexington and Concord, engulfed the hapless Lord Dunmore aboard a British man-of-war in Norfolk harbor, and buoyed state legislators who voted to expunge prewar debts to London merchants. Justice? Not if your name was John Mein in Boston or James Murray in Williamsburg.

I am making this point about public opinion since that vital element, along with a certain amount of historical mythology later buttressed by the law, explains how we have our rights as set forth in the Virginia Declaration of Rights, in our federal Bill of Rights—or in the latest opinion of the Supreme Court involving the First Amendment. James Madison's countrymen had a clear perception of God-given rights and of wrongs. Eight years of war took care of the wrongs, but two centuries later we are not as sure as they were about the rights. What is a citizen entitled to beyond the basic rights to life, liberty, and the pursuit of happiness? Would James Madison have considered hanging a convicted felon cruel and unusual punishment? Obviously he would not—yet our views on social issues have changed so much that the historical context of our Bill of Rights is often ignored in the name of compassion or modernity.

Were the Founding Fathers without a sense of compassion? Certainly not. There are no reports of capital punishment for the farm boys who resisted military drafts during the Revolution; no executions attended Shays's Rebellion; the Whiskey Rebellion came and went without a single hangman's noose tightened. Public opinion would not support summary executions of citizens who had committed no crime except that of resistance to authority. When public opinion supported the draft resisters of the 1770s, it was as powerful as the national frame of mind that approved their punishment in 1917.

There is, therefore, much truth to the argument that the Constitution is a living, breathing document. Of course, George Mason would have had Miranda shot, but we have learned a great deal about law and human rights since the eighth article of the Virginia Declaration of Rights was read by the clerk in May 1776: "A man hath a right to demand the cause and nature of his accusation . . . nor can he be compelled to give evidence against himself."[10] This is the same George Mason who saw to it that a runaway slave had his ear nailed to a post and then cut off for punishment.[11] Lest we shudder and wonder how Mason could have done such a thing, remember that he could have sought much worse punishment. In a society with few jails and fewer jailers, it was much simpler to nick an ear or flog a back than to build a jailhouse. The reformer Beccaria's teachings to the contrary, leaders in 1776 had a strong sense of the rights connected with property. The Society for the Prevention of Cruelty to Animals may wince at Jefferson's order to kill the dogs at Monticello, but dogs killed sheep, and sheep cost money. Slaves were a capital investment; dogs were a threat to livestock. To judge Mason and Jefferson by our standards is to disregard the historical perspective required if we are to understand the ordeals of human experience.

## Freedom of Conscience Underpins All Liberty

From this background of some violence we see two of the three great architects of our modern Bill of Rights who in their own day were exponents of humanitarian thought. Nursed in the lessons of the Glorious Revolution, Mason with Jefferson and Madison moved to ensure for "unborn Generations" of Americans the rights they believed were naturally bestowed on Englishmen "and ought of Right to be as fully enjoyed [in America], as if we still continued within the Realm of England."[12] Among this trio there was remarkable unity on one point in the catalog of human rights—freedom of conscience

---

[10] A. E. Dick Howard, *Commentaries on the Constitution of Virginia*, 2 vols. (Charlottesville, Va.: University Press of Virginia, 1974), vol. 1, pp. 94–95.

[11] Fairfax County, Virginia, Court Record Book, 1754, p. 72.

[12] George Mason, *The Papers of George Mason*, ed. Robert A. Rutland, 3 vols. (Chapel Hill: University of North Carolina Press, 1970), vol. 1, p. 201.

—and their concern left benchmarks in 1776, 1786, and 1791 that have spared our nation untold misery.

Madison, just out of Princeton, had been shocked by the excessive restraints imposed on dissenters in his native state, and he complained to a friend in Philadelphia:

> I want again to breathe your free Air. . . . I have indeed as good an Atmosphere at home as the Climate will allow: but have nothing to brag of as to the State of Liberty in my Country. Poverty and Luxury prevail among all sorts: Pride ignorance and Knavery among the Priesthood and Vice and Wickedness among the Laity. This is bad enough But It is not the worst I have to tell you. That diabolical Hell conceived principle of persecution rages among some and to their eternal Infamy the Clergy can furnish their Quota of Imps for such business. This vexes me the most of any thing whatever.[13]

Thus did the twenty-three-year-old Virginian watch with disgust as the Act of Toleration was ignored in his distant outpost of the British Empire. Two years later Madison made his first public step toward the leadership that came to a climax (in one sense) in 1789. At the Virginia convention in 1776, when Mason's article on religion promised "that all men should enjoy the fullest toleration in the exercise of religion, according to the dictates of conscience," Madison suggested changing "fullest toleration" to "the free exercise" of religion.[14] The difference was enormous, but Madison was not finished. Mason's article had allowed a citizen to worship in peace, but Mason added a phrase that struck Madison as a watering down of the whole concept of religious freedom:

> All of Men shou'd enjoy the fullest Toleration in the Exercise of Religion, according to the Dictates of Conscience, unpunished and unrestrained by the Magistrate, unless, under Colour of Religion, any Man disturb the Peace, the Happiness, or Safety of Society, or of Individuals.

Madison saw the latent danger in the clause, for hapless dissenters in his Piedmont county had been accused of breaking the peace simply by their presence. Madison coaxed and Mason gave way; the final article omitted all mention of restraints and simply called for "the free exercise of religion, according to the dictates of conscience; and

---

[13] Madison, *Papers*, vol. 1, p. 106.
[14] Mason, *Papers*, vol. 1, pp. 284, 289.

that it is the mutual duty of all to practise Christian forbearance, love, and charity, towards each other."

The established church in Virginia was already in disarray, but this provision finished it off in a way that emphasized the revolutionary character of the American Revolution. The Anglican-reared Mason, Madison, and Jefferson kept up their drumfire against a state-sanctioned religion. By 1786 the death knell of the established church had sounded in Virginia and, in time, throughout the Republic.

As we know, in the constitution-making decade that followed the Williamsburg gathering of 1776, five states came to borrow some version of the Virginia Declaration of Rights, and even in the states that enacted no formal bill of rights (for example, Connecticut) there was widespread acceptance of the principle involved. Rhode Island had no bill of rights, but daily experience made such a statement redundant. In most cases, however, a widespread diversity of sects was not enough. The people's mind rested easier knowing that their right to worship was a part of the law.

I want to stress the importance of this written guarantee of the free exercise of religion because it became the linchpin of our whole system of personal freedom. As my colleague Dumas Malone has pointed out, the early acceptance of the idea that a man's conscience must not be interfered with by the state has spared America the agonies that have long troubled humankind and are still pitting Christian against Christian in parts of the world today. "A long time was needed to arrive at the conclusion that coercion of opinion is a mistake," the English historian J. B. Bury observed, "and only a part of the world is yet convinced. That conclusion, so far as I can judge, *is the most important ever reached by men.*"[15] Bury was only reinforcing what his colleague John Neville Figgis said in another way:

> It is perhaps true to say, not that civil liberty is the child of religious liberty, but that liberty, whether civil or religious, was the work often reluctantly, sometimes unconsciously, undertaken by communities of men who had an end higher than political, who refused to submit religion to politic arguments, who fought for ends never entirely utilitarian.[16]

The Americans who drafted our bills of rights had witnessed religious bigotry in relatively mild forms. The last Salem "witch" had been

---

[15] J. B. Bury, *A History of Freedom of Thought* (London: Oxford University Press, 1952), p. 6. [Italics added.]

[16] John Neville Figgis, *Studies in Political Thought from Gerson to Grotius, 1414–1625* (Cambridge: Cambridge University Press, 1931), p. 108.

hanged in 1692, but the trials heaped on dissenters in every section of the new nation were fresh in their memories, and the lessons of history were their guideposts.

## Tolerance Spared Nation Many Ordeals

Since the energy behind bigotry is always intense, it says a great deal about the times that articles protecting religious freedom soon became a part of "the furniture of the mind" for the Revolutionary generation. Even before Vermont was granted statehood, its proposed bill of rights went into some detail to explain what the "free exercise of religious worship" entailed, including the principle "that no man ought, or of right can be compelled to attend any religious worship, or erect or support any place of worship, or maintain any minister, contrary to the dictates of his conscience."[17] And within months after Madison's version of the First Amendment was ratified, Kentucky came into the Union with a lengthy article in its constitution on religious freedom, which included the admonition "that no human authority can in any case whatever control or interfere with the rights of conscience."[18] Although the vestiges of an established church were maintained in New England until the 1830s, the public discussion and legal enactments reflected a powerful impulse toward a prevailing "live and let live" attitude in religious matters.

So it was that during a period of fifteen years the new nation had set standards for human freedom to implement Jefferson's view of why a bill of rights was necessary. Jefferson was deaf to any plea "that the only true liberty was the liberty of minority groups to be protected in their rights against the envy and malice of tyrannical majorities."[19] The people were entitled to written guarantees (beginning with the trial by jury—"this palladium" as he called it) embracing those rights that "no just government should refuse or rest on inference."

Indeed, Jefferson's judgment epitomized the whole movement to guarantee specific rights to the citizen as a shield against arbitrary rule. The Revolution was to create a government of laws, not of men, but the bills of rights became a higher law. Who was to enforce this higher law? Madison realized that the rights of a majority are scarcely

---

[17] Francis N. Thorpe, ed., *The Federal and State Constitutions . . . and Other Organic Laws*, 7 vols. (Washington, D.C., 1909), vol. 6, p. 3752.

[18] Ibid., vol. 3, p. 1274.

[19] This summary view of the dominant conservatism of the late nineteenth century historians is taken from Douglass Adair's provocative article "The Tenth Federalist Revisited," *William & Mary Quarterly*, 3d Series, vol. 8, p. 54.

ever in need of protection and saw that the special role of a bill of rights was to safeguard the minority. In *Federalist* No. 51 he spoke of the need to protect minority rights, suggesting that the solution came in the multiple interests of the majority that would "render an unjust combination of a majority of the whole very improbable, if not impracticable." After the ratification experience proved that such assurances were inadequate, to Madison himself fell the chore of introducing a bill of rights in the First Congress—a duty he shouldered in the belief that at the very least amendments protecting civil liberties would "have a salutary tendency."[20] He again referred to the danger of oppressive majorities but now saw a check in the bill of rights, which would be supported by public opinion and thus "rouse the attention of the whole community" when liberty was in jeopardy.

## Opponents in Congress Overcome

Convinced that the people supported him, Madison saw that his main difficulty was the apathy of his House colleagues. Ever the scholar, he took to scouring newspapers and pamphlets for hints in the ratification debates about what the people wanted in a bill of rights. He was greatly aided by the publication in Richmond of a booklet containing the recommended amendments from the ratifying conventions in Massachusetts, New York, New Hampshire, Virginia, North Carolina, and South Carolina. He told Jefferson the compendium contained suggestions regarding such things as contracts and paper money that really related to errors committed under the Articles of Confederation. "It is true nevertheless that not a few, particularly in Virginia have contended for the proposed alterations from the most honorable and patriotic motives; and that among the advocates for the Constitution, there are some who wish for further guards to public liberty and individual rights."[21]

Madison sifted through more than two hundred proposed amendments to settle on nineteen substantive recommendations, which he offered on June 8, 1789. He did so "that our constituents may see we pay a proper attention to a subject they have much at heart; and if it does not give that full gratification which is to be wished, they will discover that it proceeds from the urgency of business of a very important nature." He reminded the House that "a great body of the people" desired amendments and wanted Congress to act "and ex-

---

[20] Madison, *Papers*, vol. 12, p. 203.
[21] Ibid., vol. 11, p. 297.

pressly declare the great rights of mankind [would be] secured under this constitution."

Beyond the enforcement of public opinion, Madison explained, once a bill of rights was "incorporated into the constitution, independent tribunals of justice will consider themselves in a peculiar manner the guardians of those rights." The courts "will be an impenetrable bulwark against every assumption of power in the legislative or executive" branches and "be naturally led to resist every encroachment upon rights expressly stipulated for in the constitution by the declaration of rights."

Madison also spoke of the underlying presumption of his day that the state legislatures were the "sure guardians of the people's liberty." Despite this, he sought an article that would deny to any state the rights to infringe the citizen's right to a jury trial or to curb his freedom of expression. Madison made it clear that he was offering "a declaration of rights of the people" as a legislative package intended "for the tranquility of the public mind."[22] Of specific grievances he was silent, for the good reason that the dynamic new republic was lurching forward as a risk-taking, mobile society that took its freedoms for granted. The threats posed by the Alien and Sedition acts were a decade away, and one of the main freedoms that was being exercised was the right of emigration—a liberty that every American seemed to accept (and that the Kentucky bill of rights made explicit).[23]

Between Madison's first effort to obtain a bill of rights and the final ratification on December 15, 1791, the article he considered "the most valuable on the whole list" was killed in the Senate.[24] This provided: "No State shall infringe the right of trial by Jury in criminal cases, nor the rights of conscience, nor the freedom of speech, or of the press." We can only ponder the effect on our history this article might have had. Madison regretted the omission but took what he could obtain: an ironclad guarantee that the federal government would leave the peaceable citizen alone.

## No Immediate Resort to Bill of Rights

As we know, once the first ten amendments were ratified, the Bill of Rights turned into a kind of Rip Van Winkle, asleep for more than

---

[22] Ibid., vol. 12, p. 207.

[23] Thorpe, *Federal and State Constitutions*, vol. 3, p. 1276.

[24] *Annals of Congress*, 1st Congress, 1st session, p. 784; Madison, *Papers*, vol. 12, p. 344.

a century. We are familiar with the palpable violations of the First Amendment by the Congress that enacted the Alien and Sedition acts and with the frustrated Republicans who sought no court redress in 1799 because they knew what to expect from a Federalist bench. We also know that amid gag laws, burned-out newspaper offices, and violated mails during the abolitionist controversy, there was no recourse to the Bill of Rights, owing to the strong gavel wielded by public opinion along with John Marshall's opinion in *Barron* v. *Baltimore*.

In a way, Marshall gave a backhanded endorsement to the idea that states were the guardians of civil liberties: "It is a subject on which they [the states] judge exclusively, and with which others interfere no farther than they are supposed to have a common interest."[25] In this decision Marshall uses the expression "we search in vain," and truly we look fruitlessly in the early court reports for cases in which a citizen claimed he was denied a right to counsel or that he was placed in double jeopardy.[26] Not until the Fourteenth Amendment spread its broad umbrella did the Bill of Rights assume the guardianship role its authors intended. The 140 years between ratification of the First Amendment and *Near* v. *Minnesota* span a period when almost all the civil liberties of individuals were denied to citizens who were also abolitionists, religious zealots, suspected Confederate sympathizers, foreign-born members of the Industrial Workers of the World (or even obstreperous native IWWers), pacifists, conscientious objectors, supporters of the newborn Soviet Union, labor leaders, or suffragettes. After *Gitlow*, the new era began to dawn, always attended with delays and expensive litigation.

The discouraging element in the history of civil rights violations is that public opinion most often was not with the injured citizen, but was highly supportive of those willing to deny a citizen his rights on the grounds of expediency or the exigencies of the times. The flag-wavers shouted down those who refused to salute the flag until a series of Supreme Court decisions from 1946 onward began to sweep away restrictive views of the purpose of the Bill of Rights. Special-interest groups with funding from a national constituency began to challenge local law enforcement agencies, school boards, and univer-

---

[25] Barron v. Baltimore, 7 Peters 247 (1833).

[26] In the rare instances when the Bill of Rights was cited in Supreme Court cases during the nineteenth century, a matter of property was the key issue, not a civil right. An exception was 3 Howard 609, in which a violation of the First Amendment was alleged. The Court held: "The Constitution makes no provision for protecting the citizens of the respective states in their religious liberties; this is left to the state constitutions and laws."

sity control boards with mounting success—nearly always with the Fourteenth Amendment and its "due process" and "equal protection of the laws" clauses in the vanguard. The Supreme Court, so long deaf to this kind of appeal, now listened. Some say the Court even moved ahead of public opinion to offer succor to accused criminals, adamant atheists, and deeply committed civil rights advocates motivated by racial injustice.

## The Bill of Rights Today

All this is a familiar story shedding some light on our question, How does the Bill of Rights protect a citizen's liberties? We have gone through a tortuous process brought on by a global social revolution during the past thirty-five years. Some of the original meanings of the words in the Bill of Rights have been turned inside out, leaving the public confused as the articulate members of our society have written Beccaria into law at a time when Attila seems to be hiding in the alley. The whole spectrum of church-state relations, which seemed prosaic matters to an earlier generation, now raises new questions concerning parental control, corporate taxation, and the use of public funds for parochial schools. Our society, knowing that there are no easy solutions, is looking for common-sensical answers that once were found in the Bill of Rights. As each session of the Supreme Court brings new interpretations that often contradict rather than reinforce our mores, scholars of constitutional history and all citizens concerned for the well-being of our libertarian heritage must learn to use public opinion rather than oppose it. Rather than lament that pressure groups hope to coerce television networks and thus work outside the Bill of Rights, let us question whether a minority of journalistic gatekeepers, producers, and communications chieftains are not acting irresponsibly when they look only at ratings sheets and not at the common weal of the nation.

The force of public opinion gave us the Bill of Rights, and in a republic that force can never be ignored. One of the disturbing elements of our current social revolution is the sense of powerlessness many citizens profess as they see their standards erode. Has the end finally come to justify the means? The ABSCAM cases and their outcome suggest that this is the case. In such a climate of opinion, the use of entrapment, self-incrimination, and deception appears to have public approval. But the sword has two edges, and if the sordid mess of ABSCAM is a portent of things to come, the Bill of Rights must be turned into a fortress as well as a sanctuary. As in the past, the

Supreme Court and an executive branch dedicated to the preservation of our individual rights must be strong enough to withstand the vagaries of public opinion.

I am concerned about the relationship between our electronic media and public opinion concerning our Bill of Rights. The public opinion that demanded and obtained the Bill of Rights was based on much public debate, on widespread discussion and argumentation in newspapers and pamphlets. I fear that the general public today is not nearly so well informed and that apathy and indifference affect our citizenry more than at any time since 1774. The difficulty is exacerbated by what seems to be a wide difference between public opinion and the more advanced judicial interpretations of certain civil rights. More often than not, I fear, the public is becoming sympathetic when law enforcement officials complain about procedures governing arrests. In such circumstances the Bill of Rights may indeed become only a parchment barrier. I suspect our colleges and universities are much to blame. We academicians have laid little stress on civil rights and have allowed great attention to be focused on public wrongs. Great concern has been expressed for the possible extinction of the whooping crane, but we search in vain for a television commentator or news director of broad understanding who will use his powerful medium to attack the public apathy that can debilitate our Bill of Rights.

The struggle to maintain our liberties goes on in the courts, but the courtroom is not the last bastion of our libertarian heritage. If we are to remain a republic, the last resort must be to the people themselves. Public opinion gave us our Bill of Rights, and we must use this awesome weapon to maintain our freedom. The answer, dear Brutus, lies in ourselves; and the enemy, as always, is our apathy.

# 2

# The Constitution and
# the Bill of Rights

HERBERT J. STORING

The foundation of the American constitutional system was not completed, it is widely agreed, until the adoption of the first ten amendments in 1791. The absence of a bill of rights from the original Constitution had of course been a major item in the Antifederalist position.
"No sooner had the Continental Congress laid the proposed Constitution before the people for ratification," Irving Brant writes, "than
a great cry went up: it contained no Bill of Rights."[1] According to
Robert Rutland, whose book *The Birth of the Bill of Rights, 1776–*
*1791* is the major history of these events, "The Federalists, failing to
realize the importance of a bill of rights, miscalculated public opinion
and found themselves on the defensive almost from the outset of the
ratification struggle."[2] Another scholar, Bernard Schwartz, says:
"Here, the Antifederalists had the stronger case and their opponents
were on the defensive from the beginning. It was, indeed, not until
the Federalists yielded in their rigid opposition on Bill of Rights
Amendments that ratification of the Constitution was assured. On
the Bill of Rights issue, it is the Antifederalist writings which are the
more interesting and even the more influential."[3]

---

[1] Irving Brant, *The Bill of Rights: Its Origin and Meaning* (Indianapolis: The
Bobbs Merrill Co., 1965), p. 46.

[2] Robert Rutland, *The Birth of the Bill of Rights, 1776–1791* (Chapel Hill: University of North Carolina Press, 1955), p. 125.

[3] Bernard Schwartz, *The Bill of Rights: A Documentary History* (New York:
Chelsea House Publishers, 1971), p. 527.

Reprinted with permission from Kennikat Press Corporation, © 1978. This essay
appeared originally in M. Judd Harmon, ed., *Essays on the Constitution of the
United States* (Port Washington, N.Y.: Kennikat Press, 1978), pp. 32–48.

So, as the story is generally told, the Federalists gave us the Constitution, but the Antifederalists gave us the Bill of Rights. Moreover, it seems quite plausible today—when so much of constitutional law is connected with the Bill of Rights—to conclude that the Antifederalists, the apparent losers in the debate over the Constitution, were ultimately the winners. Their contribution to the scheme of American constitutional liberty seems to be a more fundamental one. Rutland puts this point well: "The facts show that the Federal Bill of Rights and the antecedent state declarations of rights represented, more than anything else, the sum total of American experience and experimentation with civil liberty up to their adoption."[4]

We all have a tendency to look at the past through the glass of our present concerns and presuppositions. That is altogether understandable; it can be given a plausible justification; it is sometimes said to be the only thing we can do. The result, however, is that we tend to speak to the past rather than to let the past try to speak to us. I want to try to reconstruct some of the debate over the Bill of Rights in a way that will enable it to speak to us. I think the result will be to show that the common view that the heart of American liberty is to be found in the Bill of Rights is wrong. That view rests, I think, on a misreading of the events of the American founding and reflects and fosters a misunderstanding of the true basis of American constitutional liberty.

To begin, we need to remind ourselves of some of the central facts about the way the Constitution was ratified. On 17 September 1787 the convention sitting in Philadelphia finished its business and sent its proposed constitution to Congress for transmittal to the states, there to be considered in conventions specially elected for that purpose. The Federalists in several states moved quickly to secure ratification. The Pennsylvania legislature began discussing the calling of a convention even before the Constitution had been acted upon by Congress and provided for a convention to meet on 21 November. Delaware was, however, the first to ratify, on 7 December, followed by Pennsylvania on 12 December. The Pennsylvania ratification was accompanied by charges of steamrolling and unfair tactics; the opposition remained unreconciled and demanded a second national convention. There followed ratification in rapid succession by New Jersey, Georgia, and Connecticut. By the middle of January 1788, however, no major state had ratified except Pennsylvania, where the opposition was still strong.

The Massachusetts convention met on 1 January, and the evidence suggests that there was probably a majority against the Con-

---

[4] Rutland, *The Birth of the Bill of Rights*, p. v.

stitution or at least that the Antifederalists were very strong. The Massachusetts convention saw intensive debate, accompanied by equally intensive parliamentary and political maneuvering. Finally, for reasons that will always be debated, John Hancock, the hitherto absent president of the convention, made an appearance and proposed that along with ratification the convention recommend a series of amendments to "remove the fears and quiet the apprehensions of many of the good people of the commonwealth, and more effectually guard against an undue administration of the federal government."[5] This proposal, supported by Samuel Adams, secured ratification in Massachusetts on 6 February by the still close vote of 187 to 168. Indeed, it is scarcely too much to say that this formula secured the ratification of the Constitution; for some version of it was used in every state that ratified after Massachusetts, with the exception of Maryland but including the crucial and doubtful states of Virginia and New York. The Constitution was ratified, then, on the understanding that an early item on the national agenda would be the consideration of widely desired amendments.

The story is completed in the First Congress. When the new government began functioning in 1789, James Madison introduced in the House of Representatives a series of amendments which, after consideration there and in the Senate, were framed as twelve proposed amendments and sent to the states for ratification. Two of these amendments (of minor importance) were not ratified by the states.[6] The others were ratified in 1791 and became the first ten amendments to the Constitution—our Bill of Rights.

The reader of the debates of the First Congress can hardly avoid being struck by the persistence with which Madison pressed his proposals and the coolness with which they were initially received. The House of Representatives was hard at work getting the government organized and underway. It was engaged in establishing the executive departments and providing for a national revenue system; the Senate was working on a bill to establish the federal judiciary (where several of the main questions raised in proposals for amendment would have to be faced). It seemed sensible to most of Madison's colleagues to concentrate on getting the government well launched, to acquire some experience in it, and to avoid a premature reopening of the divisive debate over ratification. It is true that Madison had explicitly

---

[5] Jonathan Elliot, ed., *Debates in the Several State Conventions on the Adoption of the Federal Constitution*, II, 122–23, 177).

[6] See below, note 10.

committed himself to the position that the First Congress should propose amendments to be submitted to the states; "amendments, if pursued with a proper moderation and in a proper mode, will be not only safe, but may serve the double purpose of satisfying the minds of well meaning opponents, and of providing additional guards in favour of liberty."[7] Nevertheless, Madison could have explained—altogether plausibly—to his Virginia constituents that he had introduced amendments as promised, but that they had been postponed until the House could finish the obviously more pressing business of launching the new government. Yet in the face of resistance from political friends as well as foes, Madison pressed forward. Why?

Madison's insistent sponsorship of amendments has to be seen, I think, as the final step in the strikingly successful Federalist strategy to secure an effective national government. I do not claim that this strategy was conceived at the beginning of the ratification debate—it developed as events emerged—or that all Federalists were parties to it; if they had been, Madison would not have had the opposition he did at the outset of the debate on amendments. But I think it is fairly clear that Madison knew what he was doing: he meant to complete the Federalist ratification victory, and in fact he did so.

Madison's proposals were designed primarily to prevent two things from happening. The first aim was to thwart the move for a general convention to consider amendments under the authority of Article V of the Constitution. A second convention was a favorite plan of the Antifederalists; the Federalists feared that such a convention might be—was, indeed, intended to be—a time bomb that would destroy the essentials of the Constitution. The second and related aim was to snuff out the attempt to revise the basic structure and powers of the new federal government, which was the main thrust of Antifederal opposition. All the state ratifying conventions that proposed amendments included suggestions to strengthen the states and limit the powers of Congress relating to such crucial matters as federal elections, taxes, military affairs, and commercial regulation. Madison made clear that he had no intention of proposing, or accepting, any amendments along these lines. "I should be unwilling to see a door opened for a reconsideration of the whole structure of Government —for a reconsideration of the principles and the substance of the powers given; because I doubt, if such a door were opened, we should be very likely to stop at that point which would be safe to the Govern-

---

[7] Letter to George Eve, 2 January 1789, ed. Gaillard Hunt, *The Writings of James Madison* (New York: G. P. Putnam's Sons, 1904), V, p. 320.

ment itself."[8] Madison's strategy was to seize the initiative for amendments, to use the Federalist majority in the First Congress to finish
the unavoidable business of amendments in such a way as to remove
from the national agenda the major Antifederalist objections—and
incidentally to secure some limited but significant improvements in
the Constitution, especially in securing individual rights.

Thus, on 6 June Madison offered his proposals, mustering all his
remarkable influence to urge on the friends of the Constitution the
prudence of showing their good faith and tranquilizing the public mind
by putting forward amendments "of such a nature as will not injure
the Constitution" and yet could "give satisfaction to the doubting part
of our fellow-citizens." He urged also that "it is possible the abuse of
the powers of the General Government may be guarded against in a
more secure manner than is now done, while no one advantage arising
from the exercise of that power shall be damaged or endangered by it."
"We have," he said, "in this way something to gain, and, if we proceed
with caution, nothing to lose."[9]

Secure in the knowledge of a large majority back of him (once he
could get it to move), Madison proposed amendments designed to
correct minor imperfections in the structure of government, which I
pass over here,[10] to secure traditional individual rights, and to reserve
to the states powers not granted to the federal government. These proposals were recast by the House, but little of substance was added
or taken away. A comparison of Madison's original proposals and the
first ten amendments of the Constitution shows both the value of a
serious and thoughtful deliberative process in improving the original
language and the dominance of Madison's impulse. The crucial fact is
that none of the amendments regarded by the opponents to the Constitution as fundamental was included.

Indeed, in one of his proposals Madison tried to turn the table
on the Antifederalists by using the Bill of Rights momentum to make
what he regarded as a substantial improvement in the constitutional
design. He proposed that "no state shall violate the equal right of conscience, or the freedom of the press or the trial by jury in criminal

---

[8] *The Debates and Proceedings of the Congress of the United States* (Washington,
1834), I, 433.

[9] Ibid., p. 432.

[10] Amendments were proposed (1) to insure at least one representative for each
thirty thousand people until the size of the House should reach a certain limit,
when the proportion would be reduced; and (2) to make increases in the salaries
of congressmen apply only after the next election of representatives. Versions of
these two amendments were included in the twelve amendments proposed by
the Congress, but failed to be ratified by a sufficient number of states.

cases." Admitting that many state constitutions already had such provisions, Madison saw no reason against double security. And he shrewdly observed that

> nothing can give a more sincere proof of the attachment of those who opposed this Constitution to these great and important rights, than to see them join in obtaining the security I have now proposed; because it must be admitted, on all hands, that the State Governments are as liable to attack these individual privileges as the General Government is, and therefore ought to be as cautiously guarded against.[11]

This amendment, which Madison thought "the most valuable amendment in the whole list,"[12] was eventually rejected by the Senate, as perhaps he expected it would be. It reflected, nonetheless, Madison's long-standing view that the chief danger to American liberty lay in the incapacity, instability, and injustice of state governments.

Madison's proposals were first referred to the committee of the whole house; later, after a good deal of controversy about how to proceed, they were referred to a select committee of eleven, on which Madison sat. To this select committee were also referred, pro forma, all the amendments proposed by the state ratifying conventions. But the committee reported out Madison's amendments only. The majority had now committed itself to action, and Madison's proposals were briskly moved through the House, over some objections of unseemly haste, echoing similar briskness and similar complaints in the early stages of the ratification of the Constitution itself. Attempts by Antifederalists such as Aedanus Burke and Elbridge Gerry to secure consideration of the more fundamental amendments proposed by the state ratifying conventions were courteously but firmly and quickly turned aside.

The objective of amendments, Madison had said, was to "give satisfaction to the doubting part of our fellow-citizens." But they did not give satisfaction. Burke spoke for most of his fellow Antifederalists when he contended that Madison's amendments were "very far from giving satisfaction to our constituents; they are not those solid and substantial amendments which the people expect. They are little better than whip-syllabub, frothy and full of wind, formed only to please the palate; or they are like a tub thrown out to a whale to secure the freight of the ship and its peaceable voyage." Samuel Livermore thought Madison's amendments were "no more than a pinch of

---

[11] Ibid., p. 441.
[12] Ibid., p. 755.

snuff; they went to secure rights never in danger."[13] And when later the amendments went to the states the main opposition to their ratification came not from the friends but from the former enemies of the Constitution, whose opinion the amendments were supposed to placate. Their view, generally speaking, was that expressed by Samuel Chase to John Lamb of New York. "A declaration of rights alone will be of no essential service. Some of the powers must be abridged, or public liberty will be endangered and, in time, destroyed."[14] Of course, Madison knew that his amendments would not satisfy the hard-core Antifederalists. His strategy was rather to isolate them from the large group of common people whose opposition did rest, not on fundamental hostility to the basic design of the Constitution, but on a broad fear that individual liberties were not sufficiently protected. By conciliatory amendments, he told Jefferson, he hoped "to extinguish opposition to the system, or at least break the force of it, by detaching the deluded opponents from the designing leaders."[15] However little the Antifederalist leaders ultimately relied on the absence of a bill of rights, too many reams of paper and hours of speaking had been devoted to it to make it now very plausible for them to dismiss a Federalist-sponsored bill of rights as mere froth. Bristling (pleasurably, one supposes) at accusations from the Antifederalists of lack of candor, Madison could ask "whether the amendments now proposed are not those most strenuously required by the opponents of the Constitution?" Have not the people been "taught to believe" that the Constitution endangered their liberties and should not be adopted without a bill of rights?[16] And by whom had they been taught? That liberty had never been in serious danger under the Constitution is what the Federalists had claimed; but under Madison's prodding they were now moderately yielding to their opponents' sensibilities. Those opponents could not expect to make much headway by admitting that the Federalists had been right on the bill of rights issue all along. "It is a fortunate thing," Madison solemnly declared in the House, "that the objection to the Government has been made on the ground I stated; because it will be practicable, on that ground, to obviate the objection, so far as to satisfy the public mind that their liberties will be perpetual, and this without endangering any part of the Constitution, which is considered as essential to the existence of the Govern-

---

[13] Ibid., pp. 745, 775.

[14] 13 January 1788, Isaac Leake, *Memoir of the Life and Times of General John Lamb* (Albany: J. Munsell, 1850), p. 310.

[15] Letter to Thomas Jefferson, 29 March 1789, *Writings of Madison*, ed. Hunt, V, 336; see *Debates of Congress*, I, 432–33.

[16] *Debates of Congress*, p. 746.

ment by those who promoted its adoption."[17] The Antifederalist leaders objected to what Madison had *not* included in his amendments, but they had been neatly boxed in.

In September 1789 Edmund Pendleton wrote to Madison:

> I congratulate you upon having got through the Amendments to the Constitution, as I was very anxious that it should be done before your adjournment, since it will have a good effect in quieting the minds of many well meaning Citizens, tho' I am of opinion that nothing was further from the wish of some, who covered their Opposition to the Government under the masque of uncommon zeal for amendments and to whom a rejection or a delay as a new ground of clamour would have been more agreeable. I own also that I feel some degree of pleasure, in discovering obviously from the whole progress, that the public are indebted for the measure to the friends of Government, whose Elections were opposed under pretense of their being averse to amendments.[18]

My argument thus far is that the primary significance of the Bill of Rights is seen most clearly in what it does not include. Madison's successful strategy was to finish the debate over ratification by pushing forward a set of amendments that almost everyone could accept and that excluded all the Antifederalists' fundamental proposals. There is also a more positive and substantial significance. To consider this we need to understand first why there was no bill of rights in or attached to the Constitution as originally drafted. The most obvious answer is that it was only after the convention in Philadelphia had spent three months constructing a government that it occurred to anyone to attach a bill of rights to it. By the time Mason and Gerry did propose a bill of rights on 12 September, it was clear to almost everyone that the convention needed to finish its business and put its proposal to the country. It seemed likely, moreover, despite Mason's contention to the contrary, that the drafting of a bill of rights would turn out to be a long and difficult business.

But why was a bill of rights not considered earlier? And why, even admitting that it might be difficult to draw up, could it be dispensed with? There is a bewildering diversity of arguments made by defenders of the Constitution to explain why a bill of rights was undesirable or unnecessary. These are not always consistent or very

---

[17] Ibid., p. 433.

[18] 2 September 1789, *The Letters and Papers of Edmund Pendleton, 1734–1803*, ed. David John Mays (Charlottesville: University Press of Virginia, 1967), II, 558.

plausible; but at bottom there are a couple of powerful and, I think, deeply compelling arguments.[19] The most widely discussed argument against a federal bill of rights was made by James Wilson in his influential "State House" speech on 6 October 1787. Wilson pointed to the fact that the general government would possess only specifically enumerated powers, unlike the state governments, which possessed broad, general grants of authority. Thus, in the case of the states, "everything which is not reserved is given," but in the case of the general government "everything which is not given is reserved." Once this distinction is understood, the pointlessness of a federal bill of rights emerges:

> for it would have been superfluous and absurd to have stipulated with a federal body of our own creation, that we should enjoy those privileges of which we are not divested, either by the intention or the act that has brought the body into existence. For instance, the liberty of the press, which has been a copious source of declamation and opposition—what control can proceed from the Federal government to shackle or destroy that sacred palladium of national freedom?[20]

Wilson articulated here a fundamental principle of the American Constitution, that the general government possesses only enumerated powers. It is, however, open to the objection that enumerated powers must imply other powers (an implication strengthened by the necessary and proper clause) and that a train of implied powers may lead to encroachments on state prerogatives. Madison made a kind of concession to this argument by proposing in one of his amendments that "the powers not delegated by this Constitution, nor prohibited by it to the States, are reserved to the States respectively." Attempts to insert "expressly" before "delegated," thus restoring the language of the Articles of Confederation and more tightly restraining federal authority, failed (though the ubiquitous "expressly" proved extremely difficult to eliminate from American political debate). Indeed, the House accepted Charles Carroll's motion to add "or to the people," which was presumably meant to narrow the states' claim to reserved powers.[21] Thus emerged what is now the Tenth Amendment. But

---

[19] One of the arguments made by the Federalists was that specific restrictions might imply powers not intended to be granted and that a listing of powers might endanger rights not listed. There was enough plausibility in this argument to lead the First Congress to add and the states to ratify what is now the Ninth Amendment.

[20] John B. McMaster and Frederick Stone, *Pennsylvania and the Federal Constitution* (Lancaster: Historical Society, Penna., 1888), pp. 143–44.

[21] *Debates of Congress*, I, 436, 761, 767–68.

this amendment was quite rightly seen by the Antifederalists as no substantial concession at all. It merely stated the obvious in a coldly neutral way: that what was not granted was reserved.

Losing the battle of "expressly delegated" was merely the sign of the Antifederalists' loss of the battle over the basic character of the Constitution. They threw up, however, a second, less than best, defense against the possibility of unjust enlargement of federal powers, and that was the campaign to give specific protection to especially important or exposed individual rights. This was part of the serious argument for a bill of rights, and Madison's response here was more substantial, as we have seen. The result is the prudent and successful scheme of limited government that we now enjoy in the United States, with both its Constitution and its Bill of Rights. Security is provided at both ends: limited grants of power; protection of individual rights. This scheme is well enough known to require from me little in the way of either explanation or praise. A view from the founding might caution us, however, not to exaggerate its benefits. Justice Black to the contrary notwithstanding, it is impossible in any interesting case to define the rights protected in the amendments with exactness sufficient to permit their automatic application. A bill of rights cannot eliminate the need for political judgment and therewith the risk of abuse. James Iredell, in his reply to George Mason's "Objections" to the Constitution, displayed the ambiguity, for example, of "cruel and unusual punishments" and at the same time the impossibility of exhaustive particularization.[22] Alexander Hamilton defied anyone to give a definition to "liberty of the press" "which should not leave the utmost latitude for evasion." "I hold it to be impracticable; and from this, I infer that its security, whatever fine declarations may be inserted in any constitution respecting it, must altogether depend on public opinion, and on the general spirit of the people and of the government. And here, after all . . . must we seek for the only solid basis of all our rights."[23]

It is interesting to consider what our constitutional law would be like today if there had been no Bill of Rights. Its focus would presumably be to a far greater extent than it is today on the powers of the government. We might expect a more searching examination by

---

[22] Paul Leicester Ford, *Pamphlets on the Constitution* (Brooklyn, N.Y., 1888), p. 360.

[23] *Federalist* No. 84. "It would be quite as significant to declare that government ought to be free, that taxes ought not to be excessive, etc., as that the liberty of the press ought not to be restrained." The state bills of rights did in fact contain many such "ought" statements which were intended to foster that "spirit of the people" on which Hamilton depends.

the Supreme Court of whether federal legislation that seems to conflict with cherished individual liberties is indeed "necessary and proper" to the exercise of granted powers. We might expect a fuller articulation than we usually receive of whether, in Marshall's term, "the end" aimed at by given legislation "is legitimate." Might this not foster a healthy concern with the problems of *governing*, a healthy sense of responsible self-government?

Doubtless a jurisprudence without a Bill of Rights would also have to find ways of scrutinizing the impact of legislation on the individual. How could that be done? Could the individual "take advantage of a natural right founded in reason," one Antifederalist asked; "could he plead it and produce Locke, Sydney, or Montesquieu as authority?"[24] Perhaps he could. One Federalist said that while there was no way to predict in advance what laws may be "necessary and proper," "this we may say—that, in exercising those powers, the Congress cannot legally violate the natural rights of an individual."[25] Another insisted that "no power was given to Congress to infringe on any one of the natural rights of the people by this Constitution; and, should they attempt it without constitutional authority, the act would be a nullity, and could not be enforced."[26] Such views have found expression in the Supreme Court by men who would rest their findings of governmental usurpation squarely on the inherent purposes and limitations of all legitimate, free government. "I do not hesitate to declare," Justice Johnson said in *Fletcher v. Peck*, "that a state does not possess the power of revoking its own grants. But I do it on a general principle, on the reason and nature of things: a principle which will impose laws even on the Deity."[27] And Justice Chase, in *Calder v. Bull*, insisted that

> there are certain vital principles in our free Republican governments, which will determine and overrule an apparent and flagrant abuse of legislative power; as to authorize manifest injustice by positive law; or to take away that security for personal liberty, or private property, for the protection whereof the government was established. An act of the Legislature (for I cannot call it law) contrary to the great first

---

[24] Essay by "A Farmer," *Maryland Gazette*, 15 February 1788.

[25] Essay by "Aristides," *Maryland Journal and Baltimore Advertiser*, 4 March 1788.

[26] Theophilus Parsons in the Massachusetts ratifying convention, ed. Elliot, *Debates on the Constitution*, II, 162.

[27] 6 Cranch 87, 143 (1810).

principles of the social compact, cannot be considered a rightful exercise of legislative authority.[28]

Of course, government *does* "violate" the natural rights of the individual, at least in the sense that it legitimately prevents him from enjoying the fullness of his rights. The question that always has to be asked is whether individual rights have been unnecessarily or unreasonably abridged. Such questions are not easy to answer, with or without a bill of rights. Any formulation of the standard of natural rights is problematical and obscure. But is it much more cloudy or contingent than "cruel and unusual punishment," "excessive bail," or "freedom of the press?" Would the nationalization of civil rights have been less well guided by something like Cardozo's standard of "implicit in the concept of ordered liberty"[29] than it has been by the tortuous reasoning induced by preoccupation with the issue of "incorporation?" Without a bill of rights our courts would probably have developed a kind of common law of individual rights to help to test and limit governmental power. Might the courts thus have been compelled to confront the basic questions that "substantive due process," "substantive equal protection," "clear and present danger," etc., have permitted them to conceal, even from themselves? Is it possible that without a bill of rights we might suffer less of that ignoble battering between absolutistic positivism and flaccid historicism that characterizes our constitutional law today?

I stray from my principal concern, though not, I think, from the spirit of the argument I am examining. The basis of the Federalist argument was that the whole notion of a bill of rights as generally understood is alien to American government. It was derived from Britain where there was no written constitution and where individual liberties were secured by marking out limits on royal prerogative. Here the Constitution itself is a bill of rights, the Federalists often argued, meaning that it was derived from the people themselves, that it provided for a sound system of representation, and that it granted limited powers to a balanced government. Quoting from the opening of the preamble, *Publius* said, "Here is a better recognition of popular rights than volumes of aphorisms which make the principal figure in several of our State bills of rights and which would sound much better in a treatise of ethics than in a constitution of government."[30] This argument shows the redundancy of any declaration of the right of people to establish their own government, but it does not reach

---

[28] 3 Dallas 386, 387 (1798).
[29] Palko v. Connecticut, 302 U.S. 319, (1937).
[30] *Federalist* No. 84.

the chief problem of popular government, which is majority tyranny. Protecting individuals and minorities against unjust action by the majority, or the government reflecting the wishes of the majority, is a major benefit of a bill of rights in the Antifederalist view. Like most Federalists, Madison never denied this, but he did not think it very reliable. The solution has to be found at a deeper level, in the functioning of a large, differentiated commercial society. And so far as the possible dangers from government are concerned, protection must be found in the very constitution of that government. Thus, Thomas McKean told his Pennsylvania colleagues that although a bill of rights "can do no harm, I believe, yet it is an unnecessary instrument, for in fact the whole plan of government is nothing more than a bill of rights—a declaration of the people in what manner they choose to be governed."[31] In the words of another Federalist:

> Where the powers to be exercised, under a certain system, are in themselves consistent with the people's liberties, are legally defined, guarded and ascertained, and ample provision made for bringing condign punishment to all such as shall overstep the limitations of the law—it is hard to conceive of a greater security for the rights of the people.[32]

But admitting that a bill of rights was not necessary, what harm could it do? "A bill of rights may be summed up in a few words," Patrick Henry told his fellow Virginians. "What do they tell us?— That our rights are reserved. Why not say so? Is it because it will consume too much paper?"[33] By 1789 Madison conceded this; he told Congress that we have nothing to lose and something to gain by amendments to secure individual rights. Why had he not conceded the point earlier? Madison admitted that "some policy had been made use of, perhaps, by gentlemen on both sides of the question."[34] On the Federalist side, an unyielding resistance to a bill of rights is to be explained by a fear that it would divert the campaign for ratification of the Constitution into what surely would have been a long and circuitous route to amendments, a route along which the essentials of the Constitution would have been extremely difficult to protect. As long as the Constitution remained unratified, Madison wrote to George Eve in 1783, "I opposed all previous alterations as calculated to throw

---

[31] McMaster and Stone, p. 252.

[32] Essay by "Atticus," *Boston Independent Chronicle*, 28 November 1787.

[33] Elliot, ed., *Debates on the Constitution*, III, 448.

[34] *Debates of Congress*, I, 436.

the States into dangerous contentions, and to furnish the secret enemies of the Union with an opportunity of promoting its dissolution."[35]

There was also, I think, a deeper and more positive reason for what appears to many scholars a rigid and defensive opposition to a bill of rights. The Federalists were determined that Americans not be diverted, in a more fundamental sense, from the main task of providing themselves with effective government. Jefferson, writing from France, admitted to Madison that bills of rights have an occasional tendency to cramp government in its useful exertions; but he thought that such inconvenience was short-lived, moderate, and reparable.[36] The friends of the Constitution, on the other hand, feared that an undue concern with rights might be fatal to American liberty. "Liberty may be endangered by the abuses of liberty," Publius warned, "as well as by the abuses of power, and the former rather than the latter is apparently most to be apprehended by the United States."[37] James Iredell saw in the old state bills of rights evidence that "the minds of men then [were] so warmed with their exertions in the cause of liberty as to lean too much perhaps toward a jealousy of power to repose a proper confidence in their own government."[38] The Federalists feared that Americans were all too wont to fall into easy and excessive criticism of all proposals for effective government. They saw in the arguments against the Constitution a tendency to drift into the shallow view that Americans could somehow get along without government— without the tough decisions, the compulsion, the risk that government must always involve. The main political business of the American people, they thought, was and would continue to be not to protect themselves against political power but to accept the responsibility of governing themselves. The Federalists did not deny that government, once established, may need protecting against, but they tried to make sure that that would always be seen for the secondary consideration it is. The lesson that the furor over a bill of rights threatened to obscure was, in Edmund Pendleton's words, that "there is no quarrel between government and liberty. The war is between government and licentiousness, faction, turbulence, and other violations of the rules of society, to preserve liberty."[39]

It was altogether appropriate, from this Federalist point of view,

---

[35] Letter to George Eve, 2 January 1789, ed. Hunt, Writings of Madison, V, 318.

[36] Letter to James Madison, 15 March 1789, ed. Julian Boyd, The Papers of Thomas Jefferson (Princeton: Princeton University Press, 1958), XIV, 660.

[37] Federalist No. 63.

[38] Ford, Pamphlets on the Constitution, pp. 359–60.

[39] Elliot, ed., Debates on the Constitution, III, 37.

that the Bill of Rights should have emerged from a separate set of deliberations, occurring after the Constitution had been framed and accepted and its government set in motion. Even at this point, however, the Federalist concession was less than might at first appear. We have seen that by taking the initiative for amendments Madison confined discussion to a bill of rights (plus a few, noncontroversial changes) and excluded that whole set of major Antifederalist proposals that would limit the powers of the general government or otherwise change the basic design of the Constitution. We must now see that Madison also took a narrow view of the meaning of a bill of rights as such, with the aim of preserving not only the constitutional scheme but also the vigor and capacity of government.

In their extraordinary exchange of views between 1787 and 1789, Thomas Jefferson pressed on Madison his opinion in favor of a bill of rights.[40] But the significant fact is not that Madison came to favor a bill of rights—he said truthfully that he had always favored it under the right circumstances. What is significant is the time he chose to move for a bill of rights, the kinds of rights protected, and the form the Bill of Rights took.

> I will own that I never considered this provision [of a bill of rights] so essential to the Federal Constitution as to make it improper to ratify it, until such an amendment was added; at the same time, I always conceived, that in a certain form, and to a certain extent, such a provision was neither improper nor altogether useless.[41]

Jefferson repeatedly described the kinds of protection he wanted in terms like the following: "a bill of rights providing clearly and without the aid of sophisms for freedom of religion, freedom of press, protection against standing armies, restriction against monopolies, the eternal and unremitting force of the habeas corpus laws, and trials by jury in all matters of fact triable by the law of the land and not by the law of Nations."[42] Three of these amounted to substantial restrictions on the power of government to act—the restrictions on monopolies, standing armies, and the suspension of habeas corpus; Jefferson clearly thought that they were vital barriers against govern-

---

[40] The main letters in this exchange are Madison to Jefferson, 24 October 1787, 17 October 1788, 8 December 1788; and Jefferson to Madison, 20 December 1787, 31 July 1788, 15 March 1789. These are conveniently available in Boyd, ed., *Papers of Jefferson*, XII–XIV, and in Schwartz, *The Bill of Rights*.

[41] *Debates of the Congress of the United States*, I, 436.

[42] Jefferson to Madison, 20 December 1787, Boyd, ed., *Papers of Jefferson*, XII, p. 440.

mental tyranny. It is equally clear that Madison consistently opposed all such amendments as obstacles to effective government. He did not include them in his original proposals (though there had been such proposals from the state ratifying conventions), and he and the Federalist majority beat down all attempts to secure such amendments.

There is moreover a deeper stratum in Madison's concern to prevent bills of rights from inhibiting government. The Antifederalists' advocacy of a bill of rights was concerned with more than specific protections; their overriding concern here was to make sure that government was rooted firmly in natural rights and justice. One of the confusions to the modern ear in the debate over the Bill of Rights and in the language of the old state bills of rights is the jumbling together of natural rights, civil rights, basic principles of justice, maxims of government, and specific legal protections. The state bills of rights were full of "oughts" and general principles. The Virginia Declaration of Rights of 1776 provides, for example: "That all men are by nature equally free and independent, and have certain inherent rights, of which, when they enter into a state of society, they cannot, by any compact deprive or divest their posterity; namely, the enjoyment of life and liberty, with the means of acquiring and possessing property, and pursuing and obtaining happiness and safety." Again, "Government is, or ought to be, instituted for the common benefit, protection, and security of the people, nation or community." The legislative and executive powers "should be separate and distinct from the judiciary"; "elections . . . ought to be free"; jury trial in civil cases "is preferable to any other, and ought to be held sacred."

Bills of rights were often described by their advocates as having as their purpose "to secure to every member of society those unalienable rights which ought not to be given up to any government."[43] Yet bills of rights, as we know them today, do not protect natural rights. And there seems to be something empty in the declarations of natural rights in a constitution. That was the Federalist view. Thus, the acerbic Dr. Rush praised the framers for not disgracing the Constitution with a bill of rights: "As we enjoy all our natural rights from a pre-occupancy, antecedent to the social state," it would be "absurd to frame a formal declaration that our natural rights are acquired from ourselves."[44] The Antifederalists insisted, on the contrary, that the main purpose of a bill of rights is to provide an explicit set of standards in terms of which a government can be judged and, when necessary, resisted. A good bill of rights is a book in which a people can read the

---

[43] Elliot, ed., *Debates on the Constitution*, IV, 137.

[44] McMaster and Stone, *Pennsylvania and the Federal Constitution*, p. 295.

fundamental principles of their political being. "Those rights characterize the man, essentially the true republican, the citizen of this continent; their enumeration, in head of the new constitution, can inspire and conserve the affection for the native country, they will be the first lesson of the young citizens becoming men, to sustain the dignity of their being."[45] This is what explains the affirmation of natural rights, the "oughts," the unenforceable generality of the state bills of rights and of many of the Antifederalists' proposals. In Patrick Henry's words:

> There are certain maxims by which every wise and enlightened people will regulate their conduct. There are certain political maxims which no free people ought ever to abandon —maxims of which the observance is essential to the security of happiness. . . .
> We have one, sir, *that all men are by nature free and independent, and have certain inherent rights, of which, when they enter into society, they cannot by any compact deprive or divest their posterity.* We have a set of maxims of the same spirit, which must be beloved by every friend to liberty, to virtue, to mankind: our bill of rights contains those admirable maxims.[46]

This was the reason that the state bills of rights preceded their constitutions and could be described as the foundation of government. Edmund Randolph put it as well as anyone in his comment on the Virginia bill of rights:

> In the formation of this bill of rights two objectives were contemplated: one, that the legislature should not in their acts violate any of those cannons [*sic*]; the other, that in all the revolutions of time, of human opinion, and of government, a perpetual standard should be erected around which the people might rally, and by a notorious record be forever admonished to be watchful, firm and virtuous.
> The corner stone being thus laid, a constitution, delegating portions of power to different organs under certain modifications, was of course to be raised upon it.[47]

The problem with a bill of rights as a "perpetual standard" or a set of maxims to which people might rally is that it may tend to undermine stable and effective government. The Virginia Declaration of

---

[45] *Virginia Independent Chronicle*, 25 June 1788. See *An Additional Number of Letters from the Federal Farmer to the Republican* (New York, 1788), p. 144.

[46] Elliot, ed., *Debates on the Constitution*, III, 137; see essay by "A Delegate" in *Virginia Independent Chronicle*, 18 June, 25 June 1787.

[47] Schwartz, *The Bill of Rights*, p. 249.

Rights asserted that free government depends on "a frequent recurrence to fundamental principles." The Federalists doubted that. Recurrence to first principles does not substitute for well-constituted and effective government. In some cases, it may interfere. Does a constant emphasis on unalienable natural rights foster good citizenship or a sense of community? Does a constant emphasis on popular sovereignty foster responsible government? Does a constant emphasis on a right to abolish government foster the kind of popular support that any government needs? The Federalists did not doubt that these first principles are true, that they may be resorted to, that they provide the ultimate source and justification of government. The problem is that these principles, while true, can also endanger government. Even rational and well-constituted governments need and deserve a presumption of legitimacy and permanence.[48] A bill of rights that presses these first principles to the fore tends to deprive government of that presumption.

For this reason, I think, Madison drastically limited the kind of standard-setting, maxim-describing, teaching function of bills of rights that the Antifederalists thought so important. In the hands of Madison and the majority of the First Congress, the Bill of Rights became what it is today: not the broad principles establishing the ends and limits of government, not "maxims" to be learned and looked up to by generations of Americans, not statements of those first principles to which a healthy people should, according to the Virginia Declaration of Rights, frequently resort; but specific protections of traditional civil rights.

With two exceptions, all the "oughts," all the statements of general principle, were excluded from Madison's original proposals—and these two were themselves eliminated before the House of Representatives finished its work. One of Madison's amendments would have declared that the powers delegated by the Constitution "are appropriated to the departments to which they are respectively distributed" so that no department shall exercise powers vested in another.[49] This was rather weakly defended by Madison in the House, where it was accepted; but it was rejected by the Senate, and no one seems to have regretted its loss. The second and most important residue of the old maxims was Madison's first proposal, which was a statement that all power derives from the people, that government ought to be instituted for the benefit of the people, and that the people have a right to change the government when they find it ad-

---

[48] See *Federalist* No. 49.

[49] *Debates of the Congress of the United States,* I, 435–36.

verse or inadequate to its purposes.[50] This proposal was later reduced by a committee (on which Madison sat) to a brief and ill-fitting preface to the preamble ("Government being intended for the benefit of the people, and the rightful establishment thereof being derived from their authority alone, We the People of the United States . . ."). It was finally dropped altogether as a result of the acceptance of Sherman's proposal to have the amendments added at the end of the Constitution. It is hard to imagine that Madison was sorry to see these proposals rejected. Indeed, it is curious how poorly they fit into the Constitution. The separation of powers amendment was to be given a separate article of its own, a clear breach of the economy of the Constitution; yet there was no other place for it. Even more striking is the awkward placing of Madison's first proposal prior to the preamble and the intolerable grammatical cumbersomeness of the Committee of Eleven version. Both these drafting inelegancies derived from Madison's determination to fit all of the amendments into the existing text of the Constitution.

Virtually all the advocates of a bill of rights assumed that it should come at the head of the Constitution; Madison wanted it in the body; it came finally at the tail.[51] Madison's argument was that "there is a neatness and propriety in incorporating the amendments into the Constitution itself; in that case the system will remain uniform and entire." He wanted to avoid a form that would emphasize the *distinction*, common in the states, between the Constitution and the Bill of Rights. On the other hand, Roger Sherman, who was far from keen on having amendments at all, argued that to try to interweave the amendments with the Constitution was to mix brass, iron, and clay; "The Constitution is the act of the people and ought to remain entire." George Clymer supported Sherman; the amendments should be kept separate so that the Constitution "would remain a monument to justify those who made it; by a comparison the world would discover the perfection of the original and the superfluity of the amendments."

---

[50] Ibid., pp. 433–34. Already this proposal significantly modified the language of the Virginia Declaration of Rights and the proposal of the Virginia convention, from which it was drawn, in the direction of supporting government. It does not begin, as the earlier versions do, with any declarations of natural rights of individuals; Madison's beginning point is already a society. The "inherent rights of which man cannot be divested," of the Virginia Declaration of Rights, are here converted into "benefits of the people" for the sake of which government is instituted. The right "to reform, alter or abolish government" (in the Virginia Declaration of Rights) or the rejection of the "slavish doctrine of non-resistance" (in the proposals of the Virginia ratifying convention) is moderated to a right to "reform or change government."

[51] This debate appears in *Debates of the Congress of the United States*, I, 707–17.

Madison sought to secure his amendments against the possibility of their being held merely redundant and ineffective; he wanted them to "stand upon as good a foundation as the original work." When he said that a separate set of amendments would "create unfavourable comparisons," he was concerned to avoid a denigration of the amendments. But neither did he wish to elevate them to a distinct, primary position. His proposed form was designed to secure protection for the most widely agreed rights that would be both authoritative and inconspicuous. Sherman had his way, for reasons that do not fully emerge from the report of the debate. Ironically, the result seems to have been exactly the opposite of what Sherman intended, and yet to have gone beyond what Madison wanted. Separate listing of the first ten amendments has elevated rather than weakened their status. The over-all result is a Bill of Rights that is much less than the broad, preambular statement of basic principles that the enthusiastic proponents of bills of rights had in mind. At the same time it is—or has in this century become—rather more significant (not less, as Sherman and his friends wanted) than scattered protections of individual rights inserted into the Constitution would have been.

What can we say in conclusion in answer to our original questions? What is the significance of the absence of a bill of rights from the original Constitution and of its subsequent addition?

First, the basic justification for the absence of a bill of rights was that the main business of a free people is to establish and conduct good government; that is where the security of freedom must be sought. For the Americans in the 1780s, still warm with the ultimate truths of natural rights and revolution, the rhetoric of bills of rights might serve as a delusive substitute for the hard tasks of self-government.

Yet, second, bills of rights are an appropriate second step. Governments do tend to abuse their powers; and while the main protections are to be found in representation and social and political checks, a bill of rights can provide useful supplemental security.

Third, the initiative seized by Madison in the First Congress enabled the Federalists to complete their ratification victory, by using amendments that better secured individual rights as the vehicle for decisively (if not finally) laying to rest the major Antifederalist objections to the powers of the general government.

Fourth, the traditional notion of a bill of rights was drastically narrowed by largely eliminating the usual declarations of first principles, frequent resort to which, Madison thought, caused serious harm to government by disturbing that healthy crust of prejudice needed to support even the most rational government.

At the same time, however, and finally, the civil rights that were secured by the new Bill of Rights were limited and defined enough to be capable of effective (though not unproblematical) enforcement. The oft-described transformation of the moralistic "ought nots" of the old bills of rights into the legal "shall nots" of the United States Bill of Rights *is* a true and important part of the story. But I hope it is now clear that that transformation was possible only as a result of a drastic narrowing and lowering deliberately intended to secure the central place for the establishment and conduct of free government as the main business of a free people.

Yet there is still in our Bill of Rights an echo of the earlier declarations of natural rights and maxims of well-constituted free governments. This is especially true of the First Amendment, which might be described as a statement in matter-of-fact legal form of the great end of free government, to secure the private sphere, and the great means for preserving such a government, to foster an alert and enlightened citizenry. In the form of a protection of civil liberties, then, the First Amendment echoes the great principles of natural liberty and free government that played so large a role in the state bills of rights.[52] The preamble contains a similar echo of the basic principle of human equality and popular sovereignty. The Bill of Rights provides a fitting close to the parenthesis around the Constitution that the preamble opens. But the substance is a design of government with powers to act and a structure arranged to make it act wisely and responsibly. It is in that design, not in its preamble or its epilogue, that the security of American civil and political liberty lies.

---

[52] It is of course significant in this connection that the First Amendment is addressed to Congress (the structure of the Bill of Rights is provided by the traditional legislative, executive, judicial sequence) and that for that reason, and because of the breadth of its terms, its interpretation and enforcement are unusually problematical.

# 3

# Two Models of Adjudication

OWEN M. FISS

Rights are not premises, but conclusions. They emerge through a process of trying to give concrete meaning and expression to the values embodied in an authoritative legal text. The Constitution is the great public text of modern America, and adjudication is the preeminent—though perhaps not the exclusive—process by which the values embodied in that text are given meaning. Adjudication is an interpretive process through which rights are created and enforced.

In my judgment this has always been the function of adjudication, clearly embraced and legitimated by Article III of the Constitution and continuous with the role of courts under the common law, but within recent decades a new *form* of constitutional adjudication has emerged. It is largely defined by two characteristics: first, an awareness that the basic threat to our constitutional values is posed not by individuals but by the operations of large-scale organizations, the bureaucracies of the modern state; and second, the realization that unless the organizations threatening these values are restructured, the threats to constitutional values cannot and will not be eliminated. For this complex task the traditional legal remedies—the damage judgment and the criminal prosecution—are inadequate. The injunction is the favored remedy, though it is used not as a device for stopping some discrete act, as it might have been in other times, but as the formal medium through which the judge directs the reconstruction of an ongoing bureaucratic organization.

This new mode of litigation, which I call structural reform, con-

This essay builds upon and to some extent extends the ideas contained in "The Forms of Justice," *Harvard Law Review*, vol. 93 (1979), p. 1, and "The Social and Political Foundations of Adjudication," *Law and Human Behavior*, vol. 6 (1982), p. 121. Copyright © 1984 Owen M. Fiss.

stitutes an important advance in the understanding of modern society and the role of adjudication in the larger political system. The bureaucratic character of the modern state and the public dimensions of the judicial power are properly acknowledged. But it is also important to recognize that this new mode of litigation raises a number of problems. One is instrumental. Simply stated, the question presented is how to do the job of structural reform and do it well: How shall the bureaucratic organization be restructured to remove the threat to constitutional values? A second problem, and the subject of my concern, is the question of legitimacy: Is structural reform an appropriate task for the judiciary?

The instrumental issue is of enormous importance and difficulty and must be given its due, but I believe the question of legitimacy is primary. I say this in part because I believe the dictates of legitimacy impose limitations on the means that can be used by courts to achieve their objectives. A blinding commitment to remedial efficacy, an exclusive concern with the instrumental problems, may well call into question the legitimacy of the entire judicial enterprise. ¶I am also moved by historical circumstances to focus on the issue of legitimacy.

Structural reform emerged as a distinctive form of constitutional litigation largely in response to the dictates of *Brown* v. *Board of Education*.[1] It emerged in the 1960s and reflected the special imperatives of school desegregation. Its scope was broadened in the late 1960s and early 1970s to include challenges to unconstitutional practices of the police, prisons, mental hospitals, institutions for the mentally retarded, prosecutorial agencies, public housing, and public employment. Its scope became as broad as the modern state itself. By the late 1970s, however, history took a different turn, and structural reform came under attack; today its legitimacy is being questioned with an energy and an urgency that are indeed remarkable. That questioning is not confined to structural reform, or to any particular mode of adjudication, but extends to the 1960s in general and the conception of state power implied by those times.

## Dispute Resolution and Structural Reform

The distinctive features of structural reform can best be understood by contrasting it with a model of adjudication that has long dominated the literature and is often used as the standard for judging the legitimacy of all forms of adjudication. This model, called dispute resolution, is associated with a story of two people in the state of nature who

---

[1] 347 U.S. 483 (1954).

each claim a single piece of property. They discuss the problem, reach an impasse, and then turn to a third party, the stranger, to resolve their dispute. Courts are viewed as the institutionalization of this stranger and adjudication as the process through which the judicial power is exercised.[2] Although this story is used not as an argument for the primacy of dispute resolution but only as an illustration, it does reflect the various premises that inform that model and that are challenged by structural reform.

**The Absence of a Sociology.** Dispute resolution depicts a sociologically impoverished universe. There is no room in the story for the sociological entities—social groups and bureaucratic organizations— that are so familiar to contemporary litigation. Social groups such as the inmates of a prison or patients in a hospital have no place in the story. Nor is there recognition of the existence of groups that transcend institutions, like racial minorities or the handicapped, groups whose social identity and reality are as secure in our society as the individual's in the state of nature. Furthermore, there is no room in the story for bureaucratic entities such as the public school system, the prison, the mental hospital, or the housing authority. The world is composed exclusively of individuals.

The party structure of the dispute resolution lawsuit reflects this individualistic bias; one neighbor is pitted against another while the judge stands between them as the passive umpire. The structural lawsuit defies this triadic form. Not two but a multiplicity of parties are involved. Moreover, the groups or organizations denominated parties are likely to be internally divided on the issues being adjudicated, and thus the antagonism between parties is not binary. What we find in a structural lawsuit is an array of competing interests and perspectives on a number of issues, organized around a single decisional agency, the judge.

Dispute resolution also implies a unity of functions in party structure: the plaintiff is simultaneously the victim, the beneficiary of the remedy, and the spokesperson. Similarly, in dispute resolution the individual defendant functions as the wrongdoer, as the one who bears the expense and trouble of the remedy, and also as the spokesperson for those interests. In the structural lawsuit, however, a fragmentation of roles occurs because the parties are sociological entities. The victim may be the blacks of a particular community; the beneficiaries of the decree, the entire community; and the spokes-

---

[2] See, for example, Martin Shapiro, *Courts* (Chicago: University of Chicago Press, 1981).

persons, the officers of several competing civic groups, a national civil rights organization, and various units of state and national government. We also typically find in structural litigation such participants as special masters and litigating *amici*; they are neither victims nor beneficiaries, but are often appointed by the court to represent important perspectives, sometimes of the victim groups, sometimes of the ostensible beneficiaries of the court action, otherwise likely to be slighted.

A similar fragmentation of party structure occurs on the defendant side: various entities—the school board, the housing authority, the police, for example—must shoulder the burden of remedy, and a large number of officials, local, state, and federal, must speak on behalf of all the interests affected by the remedy. Moreover, in structural litigation there is less and less emphasis on identifying the wrongdoer. Since the function of the lawsuit is not to punish nor compensate but to eliminate threats to constitutional values, the judge is able to think in wholly prospective terms. He is able to place the burden of remedy on institutions that could not properly be considered "wrongdoers," even in a metaphoric sense, but are deemed responsible for the remedy because they are uniquely able to further the constitutional values at issue. The transportation authority, for example, may not have "caused" the segregated schools in the first instance, but it may be joined as a party and required to participate in the remedy because the desegregation plan could not succeed without that participation.

In addition to altering the party structure, the introduction of sociological entities in the structural suit changes and complicates the remedial process. In contrast to dispute resolution, in which an individual is both victim and spokesperson and also the beneficiary of a court decree, the remedial task in the structural suit is much more complex because the victim and beneficiary are social groups. The judge must, for example, determine whether the victim and beneficiary groups should be coextensive and must also establish criteria for determining which individuals are to be included within those groups. Similarly, because the constitutional threat is posed by a bureaucratic organization rather than by an individual and because such an organization is likely to have an internal dynamic that at once diffuses responsibility and magnifies the severity of the threat, a remedy such as the issuance of a narrow injunction addressed to some identifiable individuals and aimed at some specific act is unlikely to be efficacious. The constitutional values can only be protected by restructuring the organization. This is a complex and difficult task; it is wholly alien to the dispute resolution model and requires a measure of activity on the part of the judge that is at odds with the picture of him as a passive umpire, simply choosing between the two neighbors. In the structural suit the judge becomes the manager of a reconstructive enterprise.

**Private Ends.** In the hypothetical state of nature where the dispute resolution story takes place, there are no public values, only the private desires of individuals—in this instance, the desire for property. Peace appears merely as a precondition of satisfying private ends. The story postulates that the judge (the stranger) settles a property dispute between neighbors, but it does not tell us how the judge resolves the dispute, only that it is resolved. The judge could even settle the dispute by flipping a coin. He may resolve the dispute according to any procedure that will minimize disputes or, more generally, maximize the satisfaction of private ends.

Structural litigation does not begin with indifference toward public values or ignorance of them. It proceeds within the framework of a constitution; and the Constitution that we know today, and that stands vindicated by *Brown* v. *Board of Education*, is a constitution that does far more than simply establish a form of government. It identifies a set of values—equality, liberty, no cruel or unusual punishment, due process, property, security of the person, freedom to speak, for example—that inform and limit the function of government and constitute the principal source of our public morality. These values transcend the private ends of dispute resolution and serve as the substantive foundations of structural litigation, which is intended to give expression to those values and protect them from the threats of the bureaucratic state.

This perspective on the social function of litigation implies that one of the central tasks for the judge is to interpret the public morality embodied in the Constitution. He does that by rendering that morality concrete and specific, by articulating what that morality means in the situation he confronts. It is here that rights are created. This perspective on the social function of adjudication also explains the remedial aspirations of the judge. His task is not to produce quiescence or peace, though that may occur and may be a necessary condition of effective relief, but rather to bring the operation of the state and its bureaucratic apparatus into conformity with the public morality. The remedy in a school desegregation suit is not intended to end the squabbles between whites and blacks in the community, though that may be a necessary condition for any desegregation plan to work, but rather to bring the school system into conformity with the dictates of the ideal of racial equality embodied in the Civil War Amendments.

In the dispute resolution story, the judge stands neutral between the ends of the feuding neighbors and is uncommitted to them: they are private ends. He is to be fair and impartial in enforcing the established rules, much as an umpire must be. In structural litigation, however, the claim is that public values are being threatened, and the judge's commitment to those values supplements his commitment to procedural fairness. He is devoted to serving public values and should be willing to rely wholly on the initiatives and strategies of the various parties, often reflecting their private motives and limitations, to vindicate those values. Additional pressure is thereby created for the judge to abandon the posture of a passive umpire and to take an active role in the proceedings, to make certain that the facts and the law are fully presented and that the defendant complies with whatever decree may be entered.

**Natural Harmony.** A third supposition of the dispute resolution story, reflecting either its individualism or its indifference to public values, is that without the intervention of courts or other government agencies, society is in a state of natural harmony. As suggested by the concept of a "dispute" itself, the story assumes that the subject of adjudication is an abnormal event that disrupts an otherwise satisfactory world. It also suggests that the function of adjudication is to restore the status quo. Structural litigation denies that assumption and reflects doubt whether the status quo is in fact just. It reflects a healthy skepticism about the existing distribution of power and privilege in American society: maybe neither neighbor is entitled to the property . . .

This skepticism helps to explain two features of structural litigation. The first concerns the requirements for initiating a lawsuit, which have generally been lowered. In the structural context, requirements concerning pleading have become more liberalized, and access to discovery has become freer: it is unnecessary for the plaintiff to be fully informed of the facts before filing the suit, and once the suit is filed, far-reaching discovery mechanisms become available, not simply for the parties to exchange information but to allow the plaintiff to investigate and substantiate his claims. Doctrines concerning standing have also become more permissive and objections of mootness less decisive. These developments reflect a growing distrust of the premise of the dispute resolution story that posits a harmonious and just status quo; the need for judicial intervention is no longer seen as an aberration, and procedural rules that require the plaintiff to be aggrieved and to present an actual controversy have been adjusted to facilitate the challenge to the status quo.

Doubts about the justice of the status quo are also reflected in the special nature of the remedial process. The goal of dispute resolution is to set things back to "normal"; the remedy is short and discrete because it simply undertakes to reestablish the world that existed before the dispute. But this is clearly not a valid conception of the remedial process in structural reform because the goal of that process is to create a *new* status quo. Restructuring a prison or a school system cannot be understood as an attempt to return to a world that existed before some dispute; it is an attempt to construct a new social reality, one that will be more nearly in accord with our constitutional ideals. And the judiciary's commitment to monitor the remedy may have to last almost as long as the social reality that the remedy seeks to create.

**Isolation of the Judiciary.** The dispute resolution model also depicts the judiciary as an isolated institution. The courts are not viewed as an integral part of a government. The quarreling neighbors ask the stranger—any stranger—to resolve their dispute. This mythical account of the process by which courts are created implies that courts can be understood apart from the larger system of government. It also suggests that the legitimacy of courts is derived from the consent of the citizenry specifically conferred on the courts as an institution. The neighbors agree to take the dispute to the stranger and to abide by his decision. The legitimacy of the judiciary stems from this initial agreement between the neighbors.

In modern society, this act of conferring authority on the judiciary through agreement among the disputants is impossible to imagine, but the consensual foundation of judicial power is nevertheless preserved through more subtle forms. Professor Lon Fuller, for example, tries to found the legitimacy of adjudication on the individual's right of participation in that process, a right that might be viewed as a way of guaranteeing a highly individual though somewhat attenuated form of consent.[3] The right of the individual to participate in adjudication is the source of its legitimacy, just as the right to vote legitimates legislation and the right to bargain legitimates contracts. Other scholars, reflecting the *Carolene Products*[4] tradition,

---

[3] Lon Fuller, "The Forms and Limits of Adjudication," *Harvard Law Review*, vol. 92 (1978), p. 353.

[4] United States v. Carolene Products Co., 304 U.S. 144, 152–53 n. 4 (1938).

have attempted to found legitimacy on the ability of courts to represent the disenfranchised and powerless as a means of perfecting the political process whereby American society as a collectivity consents to its government.[5]

In my view, courts should be viewed not in isolation but as a coordinate source of governmental power, as an integral part of the larger political system. Democracy does in fact commit us to consent as the foundation of legitimacy, but that consent is not granted separately to individual institutions. It extends to the system of governance as a whole. Although the legitimacy of the system depends on the people's consent, an institution within the system does not depend on popular consent, either in the individualized sense suggested by Fuller or in the collective sense suggested by the *Carolene Products* tradition. Rather the legitimacy of a particular governmental institution stems from its capacity to perform a distinctive social function within the larger political system. In America the legitimacy of the courts and the power judges exercise in structural reform, or for that matter in any type of constitutional litigation, are founded on the unique competence of the judiciary to perform a distinctive social function, which is, as I have suggested, to give concrete meaning and application to the public values embodied in an authoritative legal text such as the Constitution.

It is not at all necessary, when speaking of this special competence of the judiciary, to ascribe to judges the wisdom of philosopher-kings. The capacity of judges to give meaning to public values turns not on some personal moral expertise, of which they have none, but on the process that limits their exercise of power and constitutes the method by which a public morality must be construed. One feature of that process is the dialogue judges must conduct: they must listen to all grievances, hear a wide range of interests, speak back, and assume individual responsibility for what they say. Another is independence: the judge must remain independent of the desires or preferences both of the body politic and of the particular contestants before the bench. Other agencies may engage in dialogue and may achieve a measure of political independence, but this is the process preeminently and traditionally identified with the judiciary and the source of its claim to competence. It is the foundation of judicial authority.

In this scheme, popular consent to a specific institution is minimized. The judiciary's competence and thus its legitimacy depend on

---

[5] John H. Ely, *Democracy and Distrust* (Cambridge, Mass.: Harvard University Press, 1980).

adherence to these two qualities of process—dialogue and independence—not on the willingness of the people to consent to particular outcomes or on their capacity to appoint and remove from office those who exercise the judicial power. The people's consent is required to legitimate the larger political system, of which the judiciary is an integral part, and the capacity of the people to respond to judicial decisions—for example, through constitutional amendments—preserves the consensual character of the system as a whole. A tighter, more particularized dependence on popular consent would deprive the judiciary of its independence and thus its competence to speak the law.

## Threats to the Legitimacy of Structural Reform

The dispute resolution model is at odds with the social and political reality of modern society, and yet it has rebounded from relative invisibility in the 1960s to enjoy a renewed popularity in the 1980s. This resurgence cannot be attributed to the rather banal poetry of the dispute resolution story or even to some nostalgic longing it may evoke for an oversimplified world. The resurgence is, I believe, due to the internal contradictions engendered by structural reform and also to the emergence of a vision of social life that privatizes all ends.

**Internal Contradictions.** At the heart of structural reform is a conception of the judiciary as a coordinate source of governmental power that derives its legitimacy from a distinctive process. The authority of the judges to give constitutional values their meaning stems from the independence of the judiciary and the willingness of judges to engage in a special dialogue over that meaning. Structural reform rests on this perception: judges engaged in structural reform invoke the interpretive authority that is traditionally possessed by all judges and that is derived from the process through which they exercise power. At the same time, however, the distinctive remedial aspects of structural reform may impair the capacity of the judiciary to adhere to the dictates of that legitimating process and thus create questions about the appropriateness of engaging in structural reform at all.

The distinctive process of the judiciary—dialogue and independence—gives judges a special competence to interpret the public morality of the Constitution, to declare rights, but there is no general connection between that process and the effort needed to transform social reality so that it comports with that morality, to provide a remedy. The judiciary claims no special competence to make the instrumental judgments that are so pervasive in providing a remedy. The duty of formulating and implementing a remedy is, instead, entrusted to the judiciary as a way of ensuring the integrity of the judicial interpretation, since the meaning of a value derives from its concrete embodiment in practical reality (the remedy), as well as from its intellectual articulation (the right).

In dispute resolution, this allocation of power is not of any special moment, nor is the underlying theory tested, for the remedy is essentially nominal. Right and remedy virtually collapse into one: the task of the judge is to decide who is entitled to the property, and the declaration of right constitutes the remedy. The only further task of the judge is to see to it that his declaration is obeyed. In structural reform, however, the judiciary seeks to reconstruct a bureaucratic organization, and the distinction between right and remedy is sharpened. The remedial phase of the litigation takes on increasing significance and, in fact, tends to dwarf the phase in which the right is declared, at least in time, energy, and sheer intellectual absorption. The remedy often becomes the centerpiece of the litigation and the very special object of criticism and resistance.

To be sure, the judge engaged in structural reform is able to defend his authority to make instrumental judgments on the theory that such judgments are necessary to give practical effect to the right, which admittedly he is specially competent to declare; but at some point in this process, as the remedial phase grows and grows in importance, the underlying justification for entrusting him with instrumental judgments begins to seem strained. It is not that the judge is usurping the authority of some other agency, for in truth no one possesses much expertise on how to reconstruct a bureaucratic organization, but the judge must still find a source of authority for his directives. The challenge to judicial legitimacy is not one of comparative competence, but rather asks whether the judge has any authority of his own to issue his commands.

The challenge to legitimacy also arises from several dynamics created by structural reform, which tend to interfere with the process that gives courts their competence in the declaration of rights in the first place. One such dynamic, the bureaucratization of the judiciary, may be present in all forms of adjudication—for example, through the proliferation of law clerks—but it is particularly acute in structural reform because of the distinctive remedial aspirations of that form of litigation. The judge, seeking to reorganize a state administrative bureaucracy, such as an urban public school or a state prison system, often creates various adjunct institutions—special masters, for example—to formulate or implement remedial plans and to make suggestions for their modification. Sometimes the intention is to tap sources of expertise, sometimes to present views not otherwise heard, sometimes to relieve the judge of the tedium necessarily involved in monitoring the performance of a bureaucratic organization, and sometimes to act as a political lightning rod, to insulate the judge from the criticism that invariably attends any significant change in the status quo. The emergence of adjunct institutions in structural reform is therefore understandable enough, but the risk is ever present that their proliferation will fragment and blur responsibility: as the judge is surrounded by adjunct institutions, all of whom share in the decisional process in various ways, it will be difficult to believe that he is truly listening or responding to the grievance or is assuming individual responsibility for the response. The quality of dialogue will disintegrate.

Structural reform may also create a special relation between the judge and the newly reconstructed institution that will compromise his independence. Since the judge serves as both architect and structural engineer in the reconstruction of an institution, he is likely to lose his detachment from it. The reconstructed institution is largely his creation, and he may well view challenges to it as challenges to him and his authority. Another threat to independence may arise from the need of the judge to engage in politics to make his remedy effective. Judges are not all-powerful, and, given the complex and far-reaching aspirations of the structural remedy and its dependence on the cooperation of many individuals and agencies, the danger is ever present that judges will temper their idealism and their commitment to justice by what is realistic. They will negotiate; they will bargain; they will become adaptive. To make a desegregation plan work, for example, the judge must transform the hostility of parents, teachers, and administrators into cooperation; he may have to goad legislators into appropriating more money. Life tenure may continue to provide him with nominal independence, but the very desire to be efficacious and the need to win broad support for the remedy may create a dependence on others that will in fact jeopardize that independence.

The existence of these dynamics in structural reform—the bureaucratization of the judiciary, the identification of the judge with the reconstructed institution, and the need for him to bargain—must be acknowledged; so must the pervasiveness of instrumental judgments for which the judiciary cannot claim any special competence. These factors strain and test the judicial power, and yet, I would insist, they do not render that model of adjudication either incoherent or beyond the reach of the judiciary. They argue for a recognition of the limits of the judicial office and the need to find ways to modulate the strains on legitimacy, but it would be a mistake to renounce the unique remedial ambitions of structural reform. Those ambitions stem from a true perception of the nature of social reality and the entirely admirable commitment of the judiciary to make that reality comport with the values embodied in the Constitution. They stem from a repudiation of the premises of dispute resolution, and that stance is not, I suggest, an act of will, a usurpation by an imperial judiciary, but a reluctant and yet inescapable duty that arises from a proper understanding of the nature of modern society and the role of adjudication in the larger political system.

**The Privatization of Ends.** The internal contradictions of structural reform are not the only threat to its legitimacy. A more basic and more pervasive threat arises from sources unrelated to the special remedial dimensions of that mode of adjudication and in fact external to the judicial process itself. It arises from the fact that the courts are a coordinate branch of government and thus subject to the forces that are affecting all forms of governmental power. The resurgence of the dispute resolution model is not an isolated phenomenon: it occurs within a larger political context characterized by a renewed interest in market economics and theories of laissez faire and more generally by a reaffirmation of the minimalist state legitimated by the theory of the social contract. This context is set by a renewed belief in the private character of all ends.

I believe it significant that the story of two neighbors fighting over a piece of property takes place in the state of nature, because it was there that the social contract was formed. We can also see that social contract theory shares the premises of dispute resolution: it too lacks a sociology, and in it ends are private, power is legitimated through individualized consent, and, at least in Locke's version, natural harmony generally prevails. The conception of government enshrined by social contract theory and preeminent in America through much of the nineteenth century—the so-called night-watchman state[6] —is the analogue to the minimalist conception of judicial power implied by the dispute resolution model. The chief end of the state in the social contract tradition is security: to develop those conditions that will allow private persons to engage in commerce and to satisfy their own ends.

During the twentieth century, particularly in the decades since

---

[6] The phrase is from Robert Nozick, *Anarchy, State, and Utopia* (New York: Basic Books, 1974).

the New Deal and World War II, America has seen the emergence of a different kind of state altogether. The state has become an active participant in our social life, supplying essential services and structuring the very terms of our existence. To legitimate that conception of government power, we had to develop a theory of consent radically different from the individualistic, unanimous consent exalted by the social contract tradition. We also had to develop a conception of social life sufficiently rich and purposive to render intelligible the pervasive and almost continuous interventions of a state committed to improving the welfare of its citizenry. That was largely the accomplishment of the 1960s.

The emergence and legitimation of the activist state in the 1960s parallels the emergence and legitimation of the new form of litigation that I have called structural reform. Indeed, one can go further and identify a common theoretical foundation for the two modalities of governmental power. Just as the dispute resolution model shares the assumptions of social contract theory and the night-watchman state, structural reform shares the political theory of the modern activist state. Both take account of sociological realities, reflect skepticism about the justness of the status quo, and constitute an affirmative use of governmental power. Both are grounded in a belief in the existence and importance of public values and a recognition of the need to translate those values into social reality through the use of governmental power. Equality was the centerpiece of the litigation of the 1960s, as it was for the legislative and executive action of that era, but equality had only a representative significance: it stood for an entire way of looking at social life. It denoted a sphere of values that are truly public, that define our society and give it an identity and inner coherence, and that are not reducible to an aggregation of private ends. Rights were seen as the concrete embodiment of these public values and, as such, an expression of our communality rather than our individuality.

Today we feel increasing doubts about that way of looking at our social life, and we are witnessing the resurgence of dispute resolution and the night-watchman state as an expression of those doubts. Both forms of government power are invoked by those who minimize the role of public values in our social life and reduce our public values to individual interest or at best individual morality. Such a reductionism seems deeply flawed; for a community cannot exist without public values, and individuality cannot exist without community. This reductionism is also at odds with the conception of our Constitution that stands vindicated by *Brown* v. *Board of Education* and the almost two hundred years of constitutional litigation—one that sees the Constitution as the embodiment of our public morality. The privatization of ends that is assumed by the broad political movements of the day would debase the great public text of modern America, the Constitution, and would undermine important and valuable institutional arrangements.

Structural reform and the activist state contemplate an affirmative use of government power to protect the values that underlie and inform our public life. They face a crisis of legitimacy because the value of our public life is denied. These institutional arrangements can survive, and must, but only if we recover that vision of American social life that proclaims the importance of the public in our individual lives. We must somehow come to understand that our individuality is vitally dependent on community and that a public life can be the source of great inspiration.

# 4

# The Constitution
# as Bill of Rights

WALTER BERNS

At a time when so much attention is being paid to the subject of
human rights and being focused especially on those countries that
do not recognize them, it is only to be expected that Americans would
be conscious of their exceptional fortune in this respect. Nor is it
remarkable that they should attribute this to the Bill of Rights, in
our day probably the most visible part of the Constitution, and to a
judiciary with the power to enforce its provisions. Soviet citizens are
not permitted to express their political opinions freely, but Americans
have the First Amendment; Argentinians were, until recently, bru-
tally tortured, but Americans are protected by the Fifth Amendment's
provision against self-incrimination; Cubans are held in jail without
trial, but thanks to habeas corpus and the Sixth Amendment's right
to a speedy and public trial, that sort of thing cannot happen to
Americans. The list could be extended until it comprised all the privileges, immunities, and rights specified in the Constitution and the
hundreds of corresponding cases in which they have been upheld or
enforced by the courts. How does the Constitution secure rights? By
delineating them in its text and empowering the courts to enforce
them. That is the usual answer to our question.

It is, for example, the answer given in the *Citizens' Guide to
Individual Rights under the Constitution of the United States of
America*, an official publication prepared by the Subcommittee on the
Constitution of the Senate Judiciary Committee.[1] After a brief intro-
duction of the sort appropriate to guidebooks—where, for example,

---

[1] U.S. Congress, Senate, Committee on the Judiciary, Subcommittee on the Constitution, *Citizens' Guide to Individual Rights under the Constitution of the
United States of America*, 96th Congress, 2d session, July 1980.

the point is made that the original Constitution specified only a few privileges or rights and that still others have their bases not in the Constitution but in various statutes—the *Citizens' Guide* proceeds to list and then to elaborate on the various constitutional provisions, most of them to be found in the first ten amendments. As Senator Birch Bayh said in his preface to the volume, the "guarantees of individual rights found in our Constitution's Bill of Rights are the very foundation of America's free and democratic society."[2] My purpose here is not so much to argue against this contention as to show its inadequacies.

I am aware that most Americans would find Bayh's statement unexceptionable, but it is, nevertheless, an unusual contention, at least in the sense of being one that demands an explanation; after all, it is not usual for an appendage to serve as the foundation of a structure. Of course, Bayh may be right in suggesting that while we owe our system of government to the body of the Constitution, we owe our liberty or our rights to its amendments. But if Bayh is right, the framers were wrong. They expected the Constitution, even without amendments, to "secure the blessings of liberty" or, they could just as well have said, to secure the rights with which all men are by nature endowed.

What is beyond dispute is the purpose of the original amendments: they were adopted to limit the powers of the national government, not of the states. The Supreme Court so held in *Barron v. Baltimore* in 1833,[3] and anyone familiar with the debates in the First Congress, which formally proposed the amendments, or with the political agitation that led Congress to propose and the states to ratify them would have to agree that the Court was correct in so holding. It was Congress that was forbidden to make laws respecting an establishment of religion or prohibiting the free exercise thereof, Congress that was not to abridge the freedom of speech or of the press or infringe the right to keep and bear arms, the national executive that was not to quarter troops in a house without the owner's consent or engage in unreasonable searches and seizures, the national judiciary that—to confine myself to the single example of the Eighth Amendment—was forbidden to require excessive bail, impose excessive fines, or inflict cruel and unusual punishments. Except for the few provisions in Article I, section 10, the Constitution contained no specific limits on the powers of the states until it was amended after the Civil War.

---

[2] Ibid., p. iii.
[3] Barron v. City of Baltimore, 7 Pet. 243 (1833).

What is also beyond dispute, although very little attention has been paid to it, is that during what is still the greater part of our history (1789–1925), the Bill of Rights played almost no role in securing rights. Before the *Gitlow* case in 1925,[4] which began the process of incorporation or absorption of the Bill of Rights into or by the Fourteenth Amendment (thereby making it applicable to the states), there were few cases involving the first ten amendments and fewer still—in fact, only fifteen—in which a governmental action was held to be in conflict with one of them. There were only nine such cases during all of the nineteenth century, one of them being *Dred Scott* v. *Sandford* (scarcely a monument to liberty) and another *Hepburn* v. *Griswold*, which was promptly overruled.[5] The religious liberty enjoyed by Americans owed nothing to judicial enforcement of the First Amendment, nor did the freedom of speech and the press; not once during those first 136 years did the Supreme Court invalidate an act of Congress on First Amendment grounds. (It did not do so until 1965 in a speech case and until 1971 in a religion case.)[6] On one occasion the Court invalidated a federal search and seizure,[7] but most of the pre-*Gitlow* cases concerned one or another aspect of the Fifth Amendment.[8] The fact is, the Bill of Rights has served (and continues to serve) mainly to secure rights from abridgment by the states and not by the federal government, the very opposite of the role the amendments were intended to play (or the role the Antifederalists expected them to have to play).

On the whole, then, history has vindicated the Federalists, who insisted that, so far as the federal government was the object of concern, a bill of rights was unnecessary. As they saw it, the threat to rights would be posed by popular majorities, and against such majorities bills of specified rights would prove (as in the states they had already proved) to be mere "parchment barriers."[9] It is therefore not surprising that as it came from the Philadelphia convention, the Con-

---

[4] Gitlow v. New York, 268 U.S. 652 (1925).

[5] Dred Scott v. Sandford, 19 How. 393 (1857); Hepburn v. Griswold, 8 Wall. 603 (1870); and Knox v. Lee, 12 Wall. 457 (1871).

[6] Lamont v. Postmaster General, 381 U.S. 301 (1965); and Tilton v. Richardson, 403 U.S. 672 (1971).

[7] Boyd v. United States, 116 U.S. 616 (1886).

[8] The exceptions were The Justices v. Murray, 9 Wall. 274 (1870) (Seventh Amendment), and four Sixth Amendment cases: Kirby v. United States, 174 U.S. 47 (1899); Wong Wing v. United States, 163 U.S. 228 (1896); Rassmussen v. United States, 197 U.S. 516 (1905); and United States v. Cohen Grocery Co., 255 U.S. 81 (1921).

[9] Madison to Jefferson, October 17, 1788, in *The Writings of James Madison*, ed. Gaillard Hunt (New York: Putnam, 1900–1910), vol. 5, pp. 271–75.

stitution did not contain a bill of rights or that the word "right" (or "rights") appears only once in its text.[10] Yet, as Publius insisted in *Federalist* No. 84, "the Constitution is itself, in every rational sense, and to every useful purpose, A BILL OF RIGHTS." We can learn something of importance about the securing of human rights by understanding what Publius meant by this statement.

## Natural Rights and the Constitution

In Article I, section 9, the Constitution contains a statement of what might be called privileges and immunities, but this did not satisfy the Antifederalists, such as Patrick Henry. In his view, the Constitution ought to have begun with a statement of general principles, or of "admirable maxims," such as that to be found in the Virginia Declaration of Rights.[11] That statement reads as follows:

> That all men are by nature equally free and independent, and have certain inherent rights, of which, when they enter a state of society, they cannot by any compact deprive or divest their posterity; namely, the enjoyment of life and liberty, with the means of acquiring and possessing property, and pursuing and obtaining happiness and safety.[12]

In short, a bill of rights containing a statement of natural rights ought to be affixed to the Constitution.

The Federalists disagreed. They were forced to concede that the Constitution might properly contain a statement of *civil* rights, and they were instrumental in the adoption of the first ten amendments, which we know as the Bill of Rights, but they were opposed to a statement of first principles in the text of the Constitution. However true, such a statement might serve to undermine or destabilize government, even government established on those principles.[13] And the

---

[10] Article I, section 8, par. 8. So far as I know, Robert A. Goldwin was the first person to remark this, in a paper presented in 1979 to the Hastings Center, Institute of Society, Ethics, and the Life Sciences, and to be published as "Rights versus Duties" in Daniel Callahan and Arthur L. Caplan, eds., *Ethics in Hard Times* (New York: Plenum Publishing Corporation, 1981).

[11] Jonathan Elliot, ed., *The Debates in the Several State Conventions, on the Adoption of the Federal Constitution as Recommended by the General Convention at Philadelphia in 1787* (Charlottesville, Va.: Michie, 1937), vol. 3, p. 137.

[12] *Ordinances Passed at General Convention . . . of Virginia, . . . in the City of Williamsburg, on . . . the 6th of May, . . . 1776* (Williamsburg [1776]), pp. 100–103, as quoted in James Morton Smith and Paul L. Murphy, eds., *Liberty and Justice: A Historical Record of American Constitutional Development* (New York: Alfred A. Knopf, 1958), p. 50.

[13] See Herbert J. Storing, "The Constitution and the Bill of Rights," chapter 2 in this book.

Constitution was indeed an embodiment of those principles; that is what Publius meant by insisting that it was itself a bill of rights.

It is a bill of *natural* rights, not because it contains a statement or compendium of those rights—it does not—but because it is an expression of the natural right of everyone to govern himself and to specify the terms according to which he agrees to give up his natural freedom by submitting to the rules of civil government. The Constitution emanates from us, "THE PEOPLE of the United States," and here in its first sentence, said Publius, "is a better recognition of popular rights than volumes of those aphorisms which make the principal figure in several of our State bills of rights and which would sound much better in a treatise of ethics than in a constitution of government."[14] It is not usually appreciated that natural rights point or lead to government, a government with the *power* to secure rights, and only secondarily to limits on governmental power. We tend to think of government as the enemy of rights, as, of course, it can be; but, according to the principles on which the United States was founded, government is first of all the necessary condition of the enjoyment of rights.[15]

To say this is not to deny the revolutionary character of natural rights or, perhaps more precisely, of the natural rights teaching. The United States began in a revolution accompanied by an appeal to the natural and unalienable rights of life, liberty, and the pursuit of happiness. But these words of the Declaration of Independence are followed immediately by the statement that "to secure these rights, Governments are instituted among Men." Natural rights point or lead to government in the same way that the Declaration of Independence points or leads to the Constitution: the rights, which are possessed by all men equally by nature (or in the state of nature), require a well-governed civil society for their security.

The link between the state of nature and civil society, or between natural rights and government, is supplied by the laws of nature. The laws of nature in this modern sense must be distinguished from the natural law as understood in the Christian tradition, for example. According to the Christian teaching, the natural law consists of commands and prohibitions derived from the inclinations (or the natural ordering of the passions and desires) and is enforced, ultimately, by the sanction of divine punishment. Here, for example, in *Calvin's*

---

[14] *Federalist* No. 84.

[15] In this section I have relied heavily on my article "Natural Rights and the American Constitution," in Leonard W. Levy, ed., *Encyclopedia of the American Constitution* (forthcoming).

*Case* (1609), is Sir Edward Coke on the law of nature understood in the traditional sense:

> The law of nature is that which God at the time of creation of the nature of man infused into his heart, for his preservation and direction; and this is Lex *aeterna*, the moral law, called also the law of nature. And by this law, written with the finger of God in the heart of man, were the people of God a long time governed before the law was written by Moses, who was the first reporter or writer of law in the world.[16]

The point has been made by leading constitutional scholars—for example, Edward S. Corwin[17] and more recently Thomas C. Grey[18]—not only that Americans understood natural law in this sense (and to support this assertion they are inclined to cite prerevolutionary cases in which Coke is quoted or accepted as authority) but that it was this understanding of natural law that was embodied in the founding principles. But they are mistaken. What they fail to understand is that natural rights and traditional natural law are, to put it simply yet altogether accurately, incompatible; to espouse the one teaching is to make it impossible reasonably to espouse the other, and in 1776 Americans espoused natural rights. Natural law according to the tradition constitutes a kind of higher law (which is how Corwin refers to it) by which one judges the justice or goodness of the positive law. But here is Hobbes on that subject: "By a good law I mean not a just law: for no law can be unjust."[19] And here is Locke: "Can the law of nature be known from man's natural inclinations? No."[20]

In the teachings of Hobbes and Locke, the laws of nature are merely deductions from the rights of nature and ultimately from the right of self-preservation. Rather than being a "higher law" as Corwin and Grey use that term, these newly discovered laws of nature are no more than prescriptions or, better, directions showing men how to escape from the state of nature or how to escape the condition that

---

[16] *Calvin's Case*, 77 Eng. Rep. 377, 392 (K.B. 1609), as quoted in Edward S. Corwin, *The "Higher Law" Background of American Constitutional Law* (Ithaca, N.Y.: Cornell University Press, 1955), pp. 45–46.

[17] Corwin, *The "Higher Law."*

[18] Thomas C. Grey, "Origins of the Unwritten Constitution: Fundamental Law in American Revolutionary Thought," *Stanford Law Review*, vol. 30 (May 1978), pp. 843–93.

[19] Thomas Hobbes, *Leviathan*, chap. 30.

[20] John Locke, *Essays on the Law of Nature*, ed. W. von Leyden (Oxford: Clarendon Press, 1954), p. 158, n. 3.

nature put them in; this must be escaped because it is unbearable—which is to say, unmodified nature is unbearable.

It is unbearable precisely because everyone has a right to preserve his own life and there is nothing to prevent him from doing whatver he thinks is necessary to secure it. The consequence is that the state of nature is indistinguishable from the state of war, where, in Hobbes's famous formulation, life is "solitary, poor, nasty, brutish, and short." Even in Locke's more benign version, and for the same reason, life in the state of nature is characterized by many unendurable "inconveniences."[21] In short, while men have rights by nature or in the state of nature, those rights are insecure in the state of nature, where, in fact, human life itself becomes insufferable.

What is required for self-preservation, the fundamental right of nature, is peace. As rational beings, men can come to understand "the fundamental law of nature," which is, as Hobbes formulates it, "*to seek peace, and follow it.*" From this is derived the second law of nature; that men should enter into a contract with one another according to which they surrender their natural rights to an absolute sovereign who is instituted by the contract and who, from that time forward, represents their rights. More briefly stated, each person must consent to be governed, which he does by *laying down* his natural right to govern himself.[22]

Locke agrees that the state of nature has a law of nature to govern the relations among men. This law obliges everyone, "when his own preservation comes not in competition . . . to preserve the rest of mankind."[23] The law of nature, therefore, dictates the preservation of everyone as well as the condition of this preservation, peace. The trouble is—although there is a degree of difference between Locke and Hobbes on this question—at a certain point peace becomes virtually impossible in the state of nature: the law of nature dictates peace, but, because everyone must be concerned first of all with himself, the law cannot be obeyed.[24] In another of its aspects, the law teaches men how to achieve peace, but the provisions of the law can be understood only by a "studier of that law,"[25] someone like Locke and those who study and master his text. What that text teaches is that men must leave the state of nature and enter a political society,

---

[21] John Locke, *Two Treatises of Government*, II, secs. 13, 124–27.

[22] Hobbes, *Leviathan*, chap. 14.

[23] Locke, *Treatises*, II, sec. 6.

[24] Ibid., secs. 12–13.

[25] Ibid., sec. 12.

which is possible only "where every one of the members has quitted his natural power [to enforce the law of nature], resigned it up into the hands of the community."[26]

In the same way, Americans of 1776 were guided by "the Laws of Nature and of Nature's God" when they declared their independence and constituted themselves a new political community. Commanding nothing, for these are not laws in the sense of commands that must be obeyed, the laws of nature (for Hobbes, for Locke, and for the Americans of 1776) point to government as the way to secure natural rights, government that derives its "just powers from the consent of the governed."

It must be emphasized that in the natural rights teaching neither civil society nor government exists by nature or in nature. By nature everyone is sovereign with respect to himself, free to do whatever in his judgment is necessary to preserve his own life. Civil society is an artificial person to which this real person, acting in concert with others, surrenders his natural and sovereign powers, and upon this agreement civil society becomes the sovereign with respect to those who have consented to the surrender.[27] It is civil society, in the exercise of this sovereign power, that institutes and empowers government.

So it was that Americans became "the People of the United States" in 1776 and, in 1787–1788, ordained and established "this CONSTITUTION for the United States of America." The Constitution is the product of the "will" of the sovereign people of the United States,[28] the civil society to which the individual and formerly sovereign persons surrendered their natural rights. They agreed to the surrender because they were persuaded that only by surrendering their rights to defend themselves could there be peace and, with peace, security for their rights.

Peace and security for rights require first of all a government with powers. "In framing a government which is to be administered by men over men," Publius said in *Federalist* No. 51, "the great difficulty lies in this: you must first enable the government to control the governed." What will be required to effect this control will vary from place to place and from time to time, and the powers to be

---

[26] Ibid., sec. 87.

[27] As Locke puts it, the individual's sovereign power is resigned "into the hands of the community in all cases that exclude him not from appealing for protection to the law established by it. And thus *all* private judgment of every particular member being excluded, the community comes to be umpire by settled standing rules." Ibid. Emphasis supplied.

[28] *Federalist* No. 78.

exercised by government will vary accordingly. This is the burden of Marshall's frequently quoted (and almost as frequently misunderstood) statement in his opinion for the Court in *McCulloch v. Maryland*. Congress's powers are given in a Constitution "intended to endure for ages to come, and, consequently, [those powers are] to be adapted to the various crises of human affairs." It is not the Constitution that is adaptable—its meaning is fixed—but the powers must be adaptable, for, as he goes right on to say:

> To have prescribed the means by which government should, in all future time, execute its powers, would have been to change, entirely, the character of the instrument, and give it the properties of a legal code. It would have been an unwise attempt to provide, by immutable rules, for exigencies which, if foreseen at all, must have been seen dimly, and which can be best provided for as they occur.[29]

Men surrendered their sovereign power to defend themselves only with the understanding that government would defend them more effectively. In civil society as in the state of nature, rights are threatened most of all by other men and by other nations, and the primary function of government is to protect men from other men and other nations. Hobbes, the first natural rights philosopher, created a sovereign—a Leviathan—who resembled nothing so much as a chief of police.

By way of summary: the fundamental human right (or in the original and correct parlance, the right with which all men are endowed by nature) is the right of self-preservation. Men enter civil society as the first step in the process by which this right can be secured. Since all are equal in respect of this right (and, on this occasion, this is the only relevant respect), each member of that civil society is entitled to one vote on the question of the form, organization, and powers of the government instituted to secure the rights of all; and since these votes must be weighted equally, it follows that the majority rules and that each must agree to be bound by the majority. (By so agreeing, each shows his respect for the rights of others.) The right to share equally in this decision is the most important human right because government is the means by which all other rights are secured. Government must possess the strength or the powers required to protect those rights against the forces that threaten them.

---

[29] McCulloch v. Maryland, 4 Wheat. 316, 415 (1819).

## Constitutional Limits on Government Power

The power exercised by civil society, that artificial sovereign created by men upon contracting to leave the state of nature, is, in principle, almost unlimited. Its single function is to institute government; acting through its majority, it is free to determine the form of government (for, as I indicated, the Declaration of Independence says indirectly and Locke says explicitly that any one of several forms of government—democratic, republican, or even monarchical—may serve to secure rights)[30] as well as the organization of that government and the powers given and withheld from it.[31] It will make these decisions in the light of its purpose, which is to secure the rights of the persons authorizing it, and, guided by theory and experience alike, it will recognize that government, too, can pose a threat to the rights of man, even a government intended to secure them. This is why the doctrine of natural rights, if only secondarily, leads or points to limitations on government; government, as Publius said in *Federalist* No. 51, not only must control the governed but must be obliged "to control itself." So it was that in 1787 "the people of the United States" decided to withhold some powers from government and, guided by what Publius referred to as an improved "science of politics,"[32] sought to ensure that the powers granted would not be abused.

**Constitutional Majorities and Single-Issue Politics.** How does the Constitution secure rights? Not, as Publius understood the problem, by a bill of rights. Historically, bills of rights have been "stipulations between kings and their subjects, abridgments of prerogative in favor of privilege," such as Magna Charta and the English Bill of Rights of 1689,[33] and their terms have been enforced, if at all, by the political power brought to bear by popular assemblies. But in the United States there will be no king to guard against; what must be feared is precisely the power of the majorities that, under republican conditions, will gain control of those popular assemblies. Everything will turn on the character of those majorities. If they are "actuated by some common impulse of passion, or of interest," they will not respect the rights of other citizens; nor will they be readily restrained by the judiciary. A Moral Majority that is allowed to become a political majority will strip the judiciary of its powers—for example, by depriving

---

[30] Locke, *Treatises*, II, sec. 132.
[31] Ibid., secs. 96–97.
[32] *Federalist* No. 9.
[33] *Federalist* No. 84.

it of its jurisdiction over certain kinds of cases. (And it is easy to see, Publius said in *Federalist* No. 78, "that it would require an uncommon portion of fortitude in the judges to do their duty as faithful guardians of the Constitution, where legislative invasions of it had been instigated by the major voice of the community.") Appropriately, the problem is best stated in the most famous paper of *The Federalist*: "To secure the public good and private rights against the dangers of [a majority] faction, and at the same time to preserve the spirit and form of popular government, is the great object to which our inquiries are directed."[34] This statement reminds us that our question—How does the Constitution secure rights?—is essentially the same question raised and answered in *The Federalist*: By what means will government be prevented from abusing the powers that, of necessity, are vested in it?

Under a popular form, and especially in democratic times, those powers will be exercised by a majority. As explained by Publius, the problem can be solved only, if at all, by preventing the formation and thereby the rule of a factious majority. This can be accomplished, and on the whole has been accomplished, by means of the institutional arrangements familiar to any student of *The Federalist*: a regular distribution of power into distinct departments, a system of legislative balances and checks, an independent judiciary, a system of representation, and an enlargement of the orbit "within which such systems are to revolve."[35] Together these institutions constitute a structure designed to ensure that the country will be governed not by simple majorities but by constitutional majorities, majorities that respect constitutional limitations that are defined by private rights.

A simple majority may be defined in the terms used by Publius to define a faction; politically, it is one assembled—by a populist or a demagogue, for example—directly in and from the people. A constitutional majority is one that is assembled in the legislature, and its constituent elements are representatives of the people. The possibility of assembling or building such a majority depends, first, on a system of representation (whose virtues and American characteristics are described in *Federalist* No. 10, as well as elsewhere) and, second, on the "enlargement of the orbit."

> The smaller the society, the fewer probably will be the distinct parties and interests composing it; the fewer the distinct parties and interests, the more frequently will a majority be found of the same party; and the smaller the number of individuals composing a majority, and the smaller the com-

---

[34] *Federalist* No. 10.
[35] *Federalist* No. 9.

pass within which they are placed, the more easily will they concert and execute their plans of oppression. Extend the sphere and you take in a greater variety of parties and interests; you make it less probable that a majority of the whole will have a common motive to invade the rights of other citizens.[36]

Republican government requires the forming of majorities, and whether or not government abuses its powers depends on the character of the majorities formed. Publius's argument is that a majority formed in a system of separated powers and a bicameral legislature is more likely to respect the rights of all the people than a majority formed in and from the people directly, especially if the members of the legislature represent a wide variety of interests and parties and especially—hence the decision in favor of fewer representatives and larger districts—if each representative represents more than one interest or party. Security for rights, as the framers saw it, would depend on the ability of these institutions or this structure to prevent divisions in which the majority and minority are divided on a single issue, especially on a moral issue.

The fundamental soundness of this constitutional plan has been demonstrated in and by our history and nowhere more dramatically than on those occasions when it has failed. The single-issue division in 1798 between "Francophiles" and "Monocrats" produced the alien and sedition laws, the latter of which especially is commonly held to be one of the most egregious denials of freedom of speech and the press ever enacted by Congress. The fact is that the record of Congress on speech and the press is not so good as the absence of Supreme Court decisions might suggest. In 1835 President Jackson called upon Congress to enact a criminal statute prohibiting "the circulation in Southern States, through the mail, of incendiary publications intended to instigate the slaves to insurrection."[37] After a long and acrimonious debate, Congress refused to enact the bill or the even more objectionable substitute measure introduced by Calhoun, but its refusal proved to be only a nominal victory for First Amendment rights. Postmasters in southern states simply refused to deliver antislavery newspapers, and no action was taken against them.[38] Then in the Civil War, when the division on the slavery issue threatened to divide the country

---

[36] *Federalist* No. 10.

[37] James D. Richardson, *Messages and Papers of the Presidents* (New York: Bureau of National Literature, 1897), vol. 3, p. 1395.

[38] See Walter Berns, *The First Amendment and the Future of American Democracy* (New York: Basic Books, 1976), pp. 119–128.

permanently, newspapers were shut down, persons were held in jail without being brought to trial, civilians were tried by military courts, and—to mention one more example of a right abridged—property was confiscated.

These systemic failures have a common cause. The denial at the beginning of the black man's fundamental right not to be governed without his consent made it almost inevitable that he would later be denied his other rights, including his right to be represented in constitutional majorities. The consequence was that he remained a slave, and, as time passed, what was required to keep him a slave was the formation of a single-issue party. The consequences of this were felt by everyone.

**Diversity of Interests and Industrialization.** All this might have been and could have been anticipated. In *Federalist* No. 53 Publius expressed his confidence that an increased intercourse among the different states would lead to "a general assimilation of their manners and laws," but it is only in our time that Georgia has come to resemble Pennsylvania and the Sun Belt, in essential respects, New England. Again in *Federalist* No. 56 he predicted that the changes of time on the comparative situation of the different states "will have an assimilating effect."

> The changes of time on the internal affairs of the States, taken singly, will be just the contrary. At present some of the States are little more than a society of husbandmen. Few of them have made much progress in those branches of industry which give a variety and complexity to the affairs of the nation. These, however, will in all of them be the fruits of a more advanced population; and will require, on the part of each State, a fuller representation.

That is, the states will in time come to resemble one another insofar as each state becomes economically more diverse. When that happens, its representatives in Congress will each represent more than a single interest. What was required for the framers' system to work was industrialization, especially the industrialization of the southern states. Only then might they escape the curse of single-interest, or factional, politics.

Security for rights depended on diversity of interests. Publius's most famous statement of this proposition is to be found in *Federalist* No. 51:

> In a free government the security for civil rights must be the same as that for religious rights. It consists in the one case

in the multiplicity of interests, and in the other in the multiplicity of sects. The degree of security in both cases will depend on the number of interests and sects; and this may be presumed to depend on the extent of country and number of people comprehended under the same government.

What Publius does not say here explicitly is that although a multiplicity of interests comes with diversity, diversity does not necessarily come with greater size. An agrarian society, even one on a continental scale, would not be characterized by a diversity or multiplicity of interests. As Martin Diamond used to say, a large Saharan republic would be divided by the Marxist-like class struggle between date pickers and oasis landholders. Diversity comes with commercialization or industrialization, and to promote this was Hamilton's purpose in the great state papers written during his term as secretary of the Treasury.

What informed the framers' constitutionalism was their knowledge, acquired from Hobbes, Locke, and Montesquieu, that security for rights would depend on their ability to devise a system in which moral differences would not become political issues. Their initial plan to foster a commercial society, with its multiplicity of economic interests, should be seen as a major element in their effort to achieve this end. In the event, as I have explained elsewhere,[39] it was James Madison (the Publius of *Federalist* Nos. 10, 51, 53, and 56) who, as much as anyone, blocked the efforts to industrialize the South and thereby diversify its interests. Thus the national government, rather than being allowed to make the effort to control events, allowed the country to drift until the passage of time brought with it not diversity within each section and thereby a similarity of manners and laws, North and South, but the most dangerous of dissimilarities. Each section came to regard the other as a moral abomination, and a house so divided cannot stand.

The framers' intention, however, was to prevent divisions along moral lines, and on the whole their effort was successful. To this end, church was separated from state, with a view, as I once put it,[40] to subordinating religion, consigning it to the private sphere where differences could be tolerated.

To the same end, the equal right to property was secured, and the "different and unequal faculties of acquiring property" were pro-

---

[39] Walter Berns, "The Constitution and the Migration of Slaves," *Yale Law Journal*, vol. 78 (December 1968), pp. 226–228.

[40] Berns, *First Amendment and the Future*, pp. 26ff.

tected. This, Publius said, was "the first object of government."[41] Not only would this cause a proliferation of the kinds of property and the interests connected with them, but it would serve to channel the passions and energies of Americans into safe activities. America's business would be business. In the large commercial or business republic, the animosities of moral factions would be replaced by the competition of economic interests, and, properly organized, this competition would be peaceful. As Adam Smith and before him John Locke promised, it would promote material growth and the prosperity in which all interests could share.

Before the foundation of this constitutional policy could be laid, however, men would have to be persuaded to pursue material ends above or before spiritual ones. To persuade them of this was part of the great modern project fostered by the new political philosophy of natural rights. Macaulay, writing 150 to 200 years after Locke and Hobbes, understood this as well as anyone of his time. The aim of the old philosophy, he pointed out, was to raise us far above vulgar wants, whereas the aim of the new philosophy was to satisfy our vulgar wants. "The former aim was noble," he said, "but the latter was attainable."[42] What Macaulay did not mention was that this latter aim was connected with a project that was not ignoble: the securing of rights or, to say the same thing, the achievement of human liberty. The American Constitution should be seen as an institutionalization of this modern project.

**Rights and the National Government.** The framers' plan for the securing of rights had still another aspect that, though closely related to industrialization and diversification, is sufficiently distinct to deserve separate treatment. The principal political decisions would have to be made at the national rather than at the state level. In *Federalist* No. 51, immediately after saying that security of civil and religious rights would depend on a multiplicity of interest and sects, which in turn would depend on the extent of the country, Publius addresses himself to the subject of a "proper federal system." In this context he scores telling points against the Antifederalists and their latter-day descendants who, through the years, have advanced the cause of states' rights. To the extent that the interests of each state are not diversified and the Union is divided into "more circumscribed confederacies, or States," he says, "oppressive combinations of a majority will be facili-

---

[41] *Federalist* No. 10.
[42] Thomas Babington Macaulay, "Francis Bacon," in *Critical and Historical Essays* (London: Everyman's Library, 1907, 1951), vol. 2, p. 373.

tated [and] the best security, under the republican forms, for the rights of every class of citizen, will be diminished." What he is contending against here is not the mere existence of the states but the existence of "more circumscribed" states, states cut off or separated from one another by legal boundaries behind which they exercise great political powers. The political decisions that affect "the rights of every class of citizen" should, to the extent possible and feasible, be made at the national level. If such a system is not established and local majorities are thereby left free to deprive minorities of their rights, the solution will be found only "by creating a will in the community independent of the majority."

There is no evidence showing that Publius here had in mind the Supreme Court, but the example he provides of such a "will"—"an hereditary or self-appointed authority"—is a fairly accurate description of the Court as it now exists; and it is altogether accurate to say that the country had initially to rely on the Court to secure the rights of minorities (beginning with the rights of the principal racial minority) from hostile state legislation. The unnoted consequences of this are discussed in the following section.

By way of summary: In *Federalist* No. 9 Publius explains why the framers were confident that, unlike governments in the past and in other places, free government could now be established in America. Recent improvements in the science of politics, he says, or newly discovered principles, make it possible to devise "models of a more perfect structure." The Constitution was seen as such a structure. An expression of the people's natural right to be governed only with their consent, it granted powers to enable the government to control the governed and, by its structure, prevented those who controlled the government from abusing these powers. A significant aspect of this structure was the size of the country: with the "enlargement of the orbit" and industrialization would come diversity of the sort of interests that can safely be represented; with industrialization (or the commercial way of life) would also come a weakening of those interests—those moral or passionate interests—that cannot safely be represented. In these ways Americans hoped to secure their rights and those of their posterity.

## Constitutional Rights and the Federal Judiciary

Among the newly discovered principles made part of the structure of the Constitution was a judiciary "composed of judges holding their offices during good behavior." Clearly the federal judiciary was expected to play a significant role in American constitutionalism; equally clearly, at least in Publius's account,[43] it was expected to exercise what we have come to call judicial review. What was not expected was the scope of this power or the manner in which it is now being exercised.

The federal judiciary was established independent of the other branches of government in order that the judges might better be able "to do their duty as faithful guardians of the Constitution"; in this capacity they were to enforce constitutional limitations against the other branches and especially the branch from which the framers feared that encroachments were most likely to issue, the legislative. When acting in this capacity, they represent the people of the United States in their sovereign or constituting capacity; or, stated differently, the power they exercise belongs by natural right to the people, who wrote and ratified the Constitution and who can amend it. (This power is exercised by the judiciary rather than directly by the people for the reasons given by Publius in *Federalist* No. 49.) The authority to enforce constitutional limitations does not "by any means" suppose a superiority of the judicial to the legislative power; it only supposes that the will of the people, "declared in the Constitution," is superior to the will of the legislature, as well as to the will of the people declared by the legislature. "Until the people have, by some solemn and authoritative act, annulled or changed the established form, it is binding upon themselves collectively, as well as individually; and no presumption, or even knowledge of their sentiments, can warrant their representatives in a departure from it prior to such an act."[44] And if the representatives of the people in their legislative capacity are bound to such limits, it ought not to require an argument to say that the representatives of the people in their sovereign capacity—that is, the judges —are bound to the same strict limits. The judges are independent, but they owe their independence to the framers' judgment that only with it could they effectively exercise the power that by natural right belongs to someone else, the constituting people. To the people of the United States belonged the power to ordain and establish the Constitution with its specified rights, and to them alone—only to the people in their sovereign capacity—belongs the power to amend the Constitution and add to or subtract from these rights. The framers would have regarded it as contrary to natural right to endow the judges with authority to "create" rights and as sheer usurpation for the judges to exercise such a power without authorization.

---

[43] *Federalist* No. 78.
[44] Ibid.

**Judicially Created Rights.** Yet not only do the judges now create rights and do so openly and avowedly—indeed, it was in the course of dissenting from a creative judgment that Justice White said that although "the Court has ample precedent for the creation of new constitutional rights [that] should not lead it to repeat the process at will"[45]—but they do so with the support of major figures in the legal fraternity, especially those who teach constitutional law and jurisprudence. The process is known as taking rights seriously, to use the title of Ronald Dworkin's influential book.[46] Unfortunately, this way of taking rights "seriously" treats the Constitution frivolously and will ultimately undermine its structure.

Almost all of the judicially created constitutional rights have been fashioned out of the language of the Fourteenth Amendment or in Fourteenth Amendment cases, cases coming to the Court from the states. It is sufficient to mention the right of privacy and the right to substantially equal election districts.[47] This is instructive because it indicates the extent to which judicial creativity is an outgrowth of, or, some would say, is made necessary by, that amendment's presumed vagueness. It is, as I have said, "an amendment seemingly worded in so general a fashion that the judges are invited to provide it with a substance fashioned from their own 'values.' "[48] But the vagueness derives from judicial interpretation, not from the text of the amendment itself.

As Michael Zuckert has demonstrated,[49] each of the three troublesome clauses of the first section of the amendment is precisely drafted and is addressed, as it were, to a separate branch of the state governments. The first forbids state legislatures to legislate in a manner that "shall abridge the privileges or immunities of citizens of the United States." And in section 5 of the amendment Congress is given the authority to define these privileges and immunities.

The second forbids state courts, whenever a "person" is brought

---

45 Moore v. City of East Cleveland, 431 U.S. 494, 544 (1977).

46 Ronald Dworkin, *Taking Rights Seriously* (Cambridge, Mass.: Harvard University Press, 1977).

47 Griswold v. Connecticut, 381 U.S. 479 (1965); and Reynolds v. Sims, 377 U.S. 533 (1964).

48 Walter Berns, "The Least Dangerous Branch but Only If . . ." in Leonard J. Theberge, ed., *The Judiciary in a Democratic Society* (Lexington, Mass.: Lexington Books, 1979), p. 17.

49 Michael P. Zuckert and Marshall McDonald, "The Original Meaning of the Fourteenth Amendment—Once Again"; and Michael P. Zuckert, "Congressional Power under the Fourteenth Amendment—The Original Understanding of Section Five." Both unpublished.

before them, to "deprive [him] of life, liberty, or property, without due process of law." This means that state courts are forbidden to sentence any person to be executed, imprisoned, or fined or otherwise to be divested of property except according to the processes of law and after a fair trial.

The third is addressed to the state executives, who are enjoined not to "deny"—meaning, withhold from—any and every person within the jurisdiction of the state the protection of the laws. The beneficiaries of this clause are described with greater specificity ("any person within its jurisdiction") because what is required of the state here is affirmative action—it must act to protect anyone who is threatened by private parties—whereas it will have already acted against and, therefore, will have identified the persons entitled to due process.[50]

If the amendment is read in this way, the only substantive clause is the first, and, if Zuckert is correct in his reading of the legislative history, it was Congress, not the Court, that was authorized to provide the substance, which it would do by defining privileges and immunities.[51] Without dwelling on the point, fidelity to the text as written would have spared us the era of "substantive due process" and its surviving progeny, "substantive equal protection"; and we would not have reason today to complain about an "activist" judiciary. Policy would have been made, and would be made, in the Congress, where, under the Constitution, policy making belongs.

---

[50] Ibid., passim.

[51] "When we remember that it was the state legislatures (along with the state constitutions) that defined the substance of the Article IV provision respecting the 'privileges and immunities of citizens in the several states,' a provision deprived of its intended effect by the existence of slavery; and that the Fourteenth Amendment reversed the priority of state and national citizenship; and that it went on to protect national citizens from hostile state legislation; and that it empowered Congress to 'enforce . . . the provisions of this article'; then it is reasonable to conclude that Congress was empowered to define the privileges and immunities that the states were forbidden to abridge. To say nothing more here, this reading of the clause would have permitted Congress to address the problem of the freedman with Lincolnian prudence: it would have been possible to guarantee him civil rights (of the sort enumerated in the Civil Rights Act of 1866) without immediately attempting to give him—while at the same time preparing him for—the full political rights of citizens. In due course, it would have been possible to grant him the 'privilege' of attending nonsegregated schools. As it turned out, the freedman got constitutional guarantees but, in practice, neither civil nor political rights until, in our own time, the Supreme Court intervened. That intervention led to our judicial explosion, just as the Court's action in *Slaughterhouse* was the condition of the *Lochner* explosion." Walter Berns, "Judicial Review and the Rights and Laws of Nature," in W. S. Moore, ed., *The Role of the Judiciary in America* (Washington, D.C.: American Enterprise Institute, forthcoming).

Unfortunately, the amendment has never been read as it is written; and the consequence has been that we have come to expect the Supreme Court to provide the rules by which the country is in essential respects governed. Perhaps the best evidence of this is contained in the text of the proposed but unratified Equal Rights Amendment: "Equality of rights under the law shall not be denied or abridged by the United States or by any state on account of sex." For the first time in almost 200 years, a constitutional provision would not specify the substance of the right or rights being secured.

In proposing this language, the Congress simply but abjectly abdicated in favor of the judiciary, as if the judges had demonstrated their ability to serve as "faithful guardians of the Constitution." But they have demonstrated no such thing, and, considering the education they receive as undergraduates and especially in the law schools, it would be extraordinary if they had. What school today offers instruction in constitutionalism or, even more important, in the American Constitution? Some, surely, but not many and, so far as I know, not any law school. Courses in constitutional law are to be found everywhere, but they are courses on the Supreme Court, the judicial process, or the judicial power and are as likely as not to be devoted to defenses of the Court's policy-making powers. It is no wonder that the judges fancy themselves authorized (and, what is more, qualified) to create constitutional rights or that they do so without regard either to the text of the Constitution—for which, in the case of the Fourteenth Amendment, our contemporary judges cannot be blamed—or for the conditions of constitutional government, and for this they can be blamed.

We are told by a famous judge writing in a prestigious law journal that the Warren Court especially should be praised for demonstrating to law students that there is "no theoretical gulf between law and morality,"[52] which means, between the law of the Constitution and the judges' morality. This is surely heady stuff for law students who may one day be judges themselves. For to allow the judges to "create" constitutional rights means to endow them with the authority to impose their "values" on the country; in practice, of course, what they will impose will be the currently fashionable "values." This practice and the contempt or disdain for the Constitution that accompanies it are nowhere better seen than in Justice Brennan's work in *Frontiero* v. *Richardson*,[53] where the issue on which the judges found

---

[52] J. Skelly Wright, "Professor Bickel, the Scholarly Tradition, and the Supreme Court," *Harvard Law Review*, vol. 84, no. 4 (February 1971), p. 804.

[53] Frontiero v. Richardson, 411 U.S. 677 (1973).

themselves divided was whether sex, like race, should be treated as a suspect classification.

> Brennan circulated a draft opinion on the limited grounds, and then he sent around an alternative section that proposed a broad constitutional ban, declaring classification by sex virtually impermissible. He knew that his alternative would have the effect of enacting the Equal Rights Amendment, which had already passed Congress and was pending before the state legislatures. But Brennan was accustomed to having the Court out in front, leading any civil rights movement.[54]

The authors of this account conclude by quoting Brennan as being of the opinion that there "was no reason to wait several years for the states to ratify the amendment"—no reason other than the fact, which Brennan implicitly acknowledged, that the Constitution *as then written* would not support the law he wanted to write.

This sort of constitutional lawmaking is given what purports to be its philosophical underpinning by Dworkin, who argues that rights cannot be taken seriously until there has been "a fusion of constitutional law and moral theory." To make it clear that he is not referring to any moral theory that may have informed the Constitution as written, he finishes that sentence by saying that that fusion "has yet to take place."[55] The moral theory that he propounds and that he hopes to fuse with constitutional law is that of John Rawls, which (at least, as Dworkin would have it) proves to justify precisely those positions that a typical liberal academician of the 1970s finds it comfortable publicly to adopt: radical egalitarianism, reverse discrimination, a narrowing if not an elimination of property rights, civil disobedience, and the like. I am not concerned here with the validity of these positions or the cogency of the arguments he uses to support them;[56] I want only to make it clear that to take rights seriously in the Dworkian sense requires the judge to ignore whatever instruction he might receive from the men who ordained and established the Constitution. This is what the Court has been doing.

In the apportionment cases, for example, and especially in those involving the second chambers of state legislatures, the Court was given the opportunity to reflect on the nature of representative government. Instead of being guided by the Constitution as elucidated

---

[54] Bob Woodward and Scott Armstrong, *The Brethren: Inside the Supreme Court* (New York: Simon and Schuster, 1979), p. 254.

[55] Dworkin, *Taking Rights Seriously*, p. 149.

[56] See Thomas Pangle, "Rediscovering Rights," *The Public Interest*, no. 50 (Winter 1978), pp. 157–160.

by the framers, the justices proceeded to misstate some American history, to utter some platitudes about representing people rather than trees or acres, and to advance the cause, which the framers repudiated, of government by simple majorities. "Logically [as if logic were the determining factor], in a society grounded on representative government, it would seem reasonable that a majority of the people of a State could elect a majority of that State's legislators."[57]

**The Formation of Constitutional Majorities.** There is a good deal more to representative government than seeing to it that everyone has a vote and that votes are equally weighed. The purpose of representative government as the framers understood it was to permit government by constitutional rather than simple majorities, majorities assembled not from among the people but, as I said earlier, from among their representatives. These will represent a variety of interests, which means that the majority required to legislate will have to be assembled, and there are rules governing this process, rules of behavior as well as of procedure. These rules encourage accommodation. For example, they require debate, which implies on the part of those participating in it a capacity and willingness to be persuaded—persuaded by another with an equal right to form the majority or to be part of it, with an equally legitimate interest, and perhaps with a superior argument. And it implies and even encourages the willingness to abide by the vote of the majority assembled. The importance of this cannot be exaggerated. Those who participate in this process are not permitted to overlook, because the rules require them to recognize, the right of every representative to be part of the majority or to overlook the fact that the purpose of forming a majority is to govern. Free government especially is not a simple business, as representatives will come to realize when they seek the consent of those with different interests. This is calculated to affect the speeches they make. Thus representative government is characterized by speech whose pur-

---

[57] Reynolds v. Sims, 377 U.S. 533, 565 (1964). If one is to judge from the holdings in these cases, and even more from the opinions written to support them, it would appear that the Court sees itself as the only legitimate antimajoritarian institution or influence in our system of government. If that is so, the justices owe it to themselves, and beyond that to the country, to ponder the framers' warnings against a reliance on "parchment barriers." Especially in the face of some of the forces unleashed by the Court's creation of additional constitutional rights—I am thinking of the self-styled Moral Majority, for example—these barriers might prove to be very fragile indeed. Even as this is being written, the Congress is considering bills to reverse, in effect, the abortion decisions, to amend the Constitution so as to permit the states to forbid abortions, and to deprive the Court of jurisdiction in a variety of cases.

pose is to gain the consent of others, and the right to speak with a view to gaining consent is given constitutional protection in Article I. This right is also given constitutional protection by the First Amendment. But from this amendment (and, in some cases, the due process clause) the Supreme Court has created an additional right: the right to self-expression. This new right has nothing to do with representative government in general or the gaining of consent in particular. By this right one may express himself by wearing obscene jackets in courthouse corridors,[58] by uttering the foulest of language in school board meetings[59] or publishing it in student newspapers,[60] or by hanging the American flag upside down,[61] wearing it on the seat of one's trousers,[62] or, under some circumstances, burning it[63]— all forms of political expression, no doubt, but not the sort of speech that is calculated to elicit consent. Nor, for that matter, is it expressed with that intention. On the contrary, it is a way of expressing contempt: for fellow citizens, for the country (Amerika), and for the very idea of representative government. By creating this constitutional right, the Supreme Court has demonstrated its ignorance of the natural rights of Americans to be governed by constitutional majorities. A people that exercises a right to express it*self* cannot form or be part of such majorities.[64]

The Court was surely not thinking of representative government or the conditions of constitutional democracy when it created the right of self-expression, or the right to disobey a *valid* criminal statute,[65] or the right to refuse, on ill-defined moral grounds, to serve in the armed forces,[66] or the right to abortion on demand, a right fashioned out of constitutional language the Court did not bother to specify.[67] It is doubtful that it was thinking of anything other than its reputation as a court accustomed to being "out in front" of the other branches of government.

The Court has done more than its share to generate the host of

[58] Cohen v. California, 403 U.S. 15 (1971).

[59] Rosenfeld v. New Jersey, 408 U.S. 901 (1972).

[60] Papish v. Board of Curators, 410 U.S. 667 (1973).

[61] Spence v. Washington, 418 U.S. 405 (1974).

[62] Smith v. Goguen, 415 U.S. 566 (1974).

[63] Street v. New York, 394 U.S. 576 (1969).

[64] See Harvey C. Mansfield, Jr., "The American Election: Towards Constitutional Democracy?" *Government and Opposition*, vol. 16, no. 1 (Winter 1981), pp. 6, 13.

[65] Wisconsin v. Yoder, 406 U.S. 205 (1972). See Walter Berns, "The Importance of Being Amish," *Harper's* (March 1973), pp. 36–42.

[66] United States v. Seeger, 380 U.S. 163 (1965).

[67] Roe v. Wade, 410 U.S. 113, 153 (1973).

single-interest groups that characterize our politics even as they make our politics more difficult. They make demands—typically moral demands—they fill the streets with their agitating, they confront one another, but they do not talk with one another with a view to gaining mutual consent. Because they do not, they tend to lose in the representative assemblies; whereupon they take their demands to the courts, eventually to the "out-in-front" Supreme Court. Here they are likely to win.

It is as if the Court is of the opinion that taking rights seriously requires it to accord to demands or wants the status of rights, as if, by natural right, a person consents to be governed on the condition that his wants be satisfied. But this is absurd because it is impossible, and it is impossible because not all wants can be satisfied. (For example, the wants of the pro- and anti-abortion groups cannot both be satisfied.) What government can promise, if it is organized properly, is that rights can be secured, by which I mean the natural right to be governed only with one's consent. Under the Constitution's system of representative government, this becomes the right to be part of a governing majority.

To repeat: while rights, properly understood, can be secured, not all wants can be satisfied. As our history attests, however, when those rights are secured, many wants are satisfied. Their satisfaction depends on their not being seen as rights.

# 5

# Subsistence Rights:
# Shall We Secure *These* Rights?

HENRY SHUE

*Choosing freedom is not, as we are told, choosing against justice. . . . If this cruel century has taught us anything at all, it has taught that the economic revolution must be free just as liberation must include the economic.*

ALBERT CAMUS[1]

## Conflict between Generations?

The list of the rights we can reasonably demand from each other changes. The list of rights we should acknowledge as genuine does not change quickly or at the whim of intellectuals or politicians. But the list—the bill—does gradually evolve, for reasons that I will try to outline. The Bill of Rights that consummated the writing of the Constitution of the United States is one of the supreme achievements of human political consciousness, and the list of rights it contains stretched the limits of what could reasonably be demanded at the time, apart from its indulgence toward slavery. But people now are vulnerable to kinds of threats and need forms of protection that were inconceivable in the

Earlier incarnations of this essay have appeared before so many lively people who have helped me with it that it long ago ceased to be my property in any interesting sense, although I take responsibility for any bad arguments not yet scotched. This version was completed in August 1982. I would like to thank critical audiences at a Third Thursday Briefing and a Workshop on Teaching, both sponsored by the Center for Philosophy and Public Policy; at the 3rd International Human Rights Teaching and Research Symposium, sponsored by the Center for the Study of Human Rights of Columbia University and the Subcommittee on Human Rights Education of the American Bar Association; at the 25th World Conference of the Society for International Development; and on the campuses of Colgate University, Northeastern University, and Virginia Commonwealth University.

[1] Albert Camus, "Bread and Freedom," in *Resistance, Rebellion, and Death*, trans. Justin O'Brien (New York: Alfred A. Knopf, 1969), p. 94.

eighteenth century. Fortunately we can in many cases secure ourselves against these threats precisely through the cooperative action permitted and required by the acknowledgment that we may demand from each other protection against them as a right. But quite a few theorists fear that this generation of rights is in conflict with the first generation of rights enshrined in the U.S. Bill of Rights. I will try to show that the second generation of economic and social rights, and specifically the basic economic rights that have now become entrenched in the International Bill of Rights, are not in conflict with the U.S. Bill of Rights and are indeed worthy additions to the family of human rights.

The International Bill of Rights consists of the Preamble and Articles 1, 55, and 56 of the Charter of the United Nations; the Universal Declaration of Human Rights; the International Covenant on Economic, Social and Cultural Rights; the International Covenant on Civil and Political Rights; and the Optional Protocol to the International Covenant on Civil and Political Rights. The Charter of the United Nations was ratified by the U.S. Senate and is, of course, legally in force. The Universal Declaration was adopted unanimously by the General Assembly of the United Nations with energetic support and an affirmative vote by the United States. The two international covenants and the Optional Protocol have been legally in force as multilateral treaties since 1976, although the U.S. Senate has yet to ratify them in spite of the fact that the United States played major roles in both their drafting and their adoption.

Even widely accepted international law is nevertheless subject to broad intellectual criticism. Perhaps in a succession of bursts of idealism, cynicism, or an unholy alliance of the two, much too much has been promised in the international documents. Perhaps the coinage of rights is being cheapened. Perhaps, in particular, acceptance of the alleged economic, social, and cultural rights endangers the status of the civil and political rights embodied not only in the U.S. Bill of Rights but also in the Universal Declaration of Human Rights and the International Covenant on Civil and Political Rights. Perhaps the economic, social, and cultural rights of the second generation—the twentieth-century generation—will prove corrosive to the civil and political rights of eighteenth-century parentage.

In this essay I shall attempt to defend only what I take to constitute the core of the economic, social, and cultural rights in the Universal Declaration and the International Covenant, without prejudice to the other rights in this broad category. These core rights I have called "subsistence rights," or rights to minimal economic security.

Subsistence includes "unpolluted air, unpolluted water, adequate food, adequate clothing, adequate shelter, and minimal preventive public health care"—in other words, for a person's subsistence to be secure the person must "have available for consumption what is needed for a decent chance at a reasonably healthy and active life of more or less normal length, barring tragic interventions."[2] In my book *Basic Rights* I have argued that the fulfillment of subsistence rights is a necessary component of the fulfillment of all other rights. Here I want to pursue the suspicion felt by some that any economic right, even a right to mere subsistence, may conflict with or otherwise undermine some other rights that are highly esteemed by U.S. citizens.

I do not pretend to discuss the strictly legal issues. Louis Henkin, one of the United States's most respected professors of the international law of human rights, has recently concluded the following:

> In the United States rights are essentially freedoms. . . . Neither the Constitution nor the economic, social, political system of the United States "entrenches" economic and social rights. . . . But the United States can insist that its people enjoy "economic and social rights" in the spirit of the Universal Declaration of Human Rights and the Covenant on Economic and Social Rights.[3]

I rely here upon Professor Henkin's judgment on the strict questions of constitutional law and take it that we in the United States "can" insist upon enjoyment of what he calls " 'economic and social rights' " in the sense that nothing in the U.S. Constitution prevents that enjoyment. But I shall suggest that it is now pointless to put economic rights in quotation marks as if they be merely so-called rights; subsistence rights at least are now as authentic, genuine, and legitimate as any civil and political right is. And the conflicts sometimes alleged by theorists between basic economic rights and basic civil and political rights are what turn out to be unreal—the basic rights of both kinds are contributory to, not competitive with, each other.

The pedigree of civil and political rights stretches further back in time than the pedigree of economic, social, and cultural rights; but the pedigree of the one is not thus any more genuine than the pedigree of the other—it is simply older. The Chihuahua was approved by the

---

[2] Henry Shue, *Basic Rights: Subsistence, Affluence, and U.S. Foreign Policy* (Princeton, N.J.: Princeton University Press, 1980), p. 23.

[3] Louis Henkin, "Economic-Social Rights as 'Rights': A United States Perspective," *Human Rights Law Journal*, vol. 2, no. 3–4 (December 1981), pp. 235–36. The full name of the covenant mentioned is the International Covenant on Economic, Social and Cultural Rights.

American Kennel Club in 1904, and the Kuvasz was not approved until 1935;[4] but this does not mean that in the United States now the Kuvasz is any less genuine a breed of dog than the Chihuahua. In *this* regard rights are the same: Degree of authenticity is in no way proportional to date of acknowledgment. The second generation is not forever subordinate to the first, like children in a Calvinist household. The question is not when subsistence rights were first conceived. It is how good the reasons are for acknowledging them—the question of substance to which we now turn.[5]

## A General Threat to Established Rights?

In the intellectual climate of the United States two doubts about subsistence rights, a general one and a more specific one, are likely to dominate. A simple general warning, which is often mobilized against any suggestion of an economic right, is that if too many different kinds of rights are acknowledged, each separate kind will come to have less value. Rights inflation will occur. The civil and political rights protected by the U.S. Constitution are of great value. We must not cheapen their coinage by giving the stamp of a right to less worthy concerns, even if they are of considerable importance.

Now, since all dollars are interchangeable and can all be used to purchase the same commodities, while different kinds of rights are not interchangeable, the analogy being invoked is weak at best and ought not to be taken too literally. The warning does have some substance, however, even if the substance may have less to do with any kind of "inflation" and more to do with a general feature of morality and legality, which is that often one can actually obtain more by demanding less. For example, a prohibition of all consumption of alcohol may not be the most effective way to produce moderate drinking. The best way to increase respect for human rights is probably to insist firmly upon a moderate and limited range of rights rather than to make an excessively long list of demands.

Although the general warning against producing excessive duties correlative to an excessively long list of rights is well taken, its specific

---

[4] *A Standard Guide to Pure-Bred Dogs*, complied and edited by Harry Glover (New York: Mayflower Books, 1982), pp. 341, 221.

[5] The chronological priority of civil and political rights can easily be exaggerated, in any case, especially when one looks at international activity. Through the International Labor Organization (ILO), established by the Treaty of Versailles in 1919, effective international cooperation on economic and social rights was underway long before effective international undertakings on behalf of civil and political rights began.

application against economic rights by no means follows. The general point is that one ought not to endanger respect for fundamental rights by demanding acknowledgment of frivolous rights—that much seems certainly correct. But that all economic rights are frivolous and only noneconomic rights are fundamental would be quite a different matter to establish. It is certainly not obvious that rights to economic subsistence, such as rights to food, clothing, and shelter, are frivolous or to any extent nonbasic; and I and others have tried to show that they are absolutely basic. In any case, for this perfectly reasonable general warning against rights inflation to count specifically against economic rights, the general warning would need to be supplemented by a specific showing that the economic rights are all optional and expendable. To my knowledge that is something no one has done.

What usually seems to happen is that people simply note that many noneconomic rights are already entrenched in the Constitution and that the economic rights would be the additional rights lengthening the list. Such an observation is simply a bias in favor of the status quo or an instance of the error mentioned earlier of thinking that degree of authenticity is proportional to date of acknowledgment.

## A Specific Threat to Rights to Liberty?

If I must somehow assist some of those who have been deprived of subsistence because they have rights that provide the ground for duties that fall upon me, I am not free to do exactly as I please with everything I own. Perhaps, then, rights to subsistence on the part of other people will conflict with kinds of liberty to which I have a right. The issue divides into two questions: Do subsistence rights conflict with liberties? and, if so, are those liberties ones to which there is a right?

First is the question whether there are conflicts. Does one person's right to food conflict with the freedom of action of the people with the correlative duties? The answer is yes, they do conflict. But then every right conflicts with the liberty of other people. Such conflict is in the nature of a right; indeed, the whole point of having rights is to limit the liberty of other people by imposing duties upon them. The rights of any one person are largely constituted by the right-based duties of other persons. The essential core of what it means for you to have a right is that you are justified in making certain demands of me. Your right-based demands upon me are restrictions upon my liberty—legitimate restrictions, no doubt, if your right is genuine, but restrictions nevertheless. Where the right is a significant one, the restrictions upon my liberty may be significant as well.

For example, your right to integrity of the person, or physical security, imposes all sorts of limits upon my liberty: I may not enslave you, rape you, beat you up, knock you down, and so on. We do not view these limitations upon liberty as onerous because we do not consider assault, rape, and so forth as morally acceptable actions. But they are morally unacceptable because they are violations of people's rights to integrity of the person. People have no right to the liberty of assaulting whomsoever they wish. This is a liberty that there is no right to exercise; indeed, it is a liberty that we are prohibited from exercising. It is a lost liberty.

Morally there is no difficulty about prohibiting what we might call the brutal liberties. But conceptually it is important to see that we *are* interfering with liberty, by declaring that there is no right to the exercise of these liberties. These liberties are prohibited to protect physical security. A right to security that entails denying any right to take certain liberties with other people's bodies is being acknowledged.

Not every liberty is a liberty to which we have a right. Any alleged right to any particular kind of liberty needs to be given its own specific justification, as does any particular alleged economic right like the right to subsistence. That people are entitled to unlimited kinds of liberty is not self-evident, and that the more rights to different kinds of liberty there are, the better, is by no means obvious. Should people have a right to freedom to pollute the air and water or a right to freedom to explore for oil in wilderness areas or to appropriate the manganese nodules on the seabed in the middle of the Pacific Ocean? I am not implying that the answers to these questions are obviously no or obviously yes. The point is that one cannot settle whether an activity is good or not—not to mention whether people should have a right to engage in it—simply by labeling it as a liberty. Any human activity can be treated as a liberty, for example, the liberty to whip your own children or the liberty to earn your living as a prostitute. Once again, I am not trying here to settle the question of whether parents should have a right to discipline their own children physically or whether a man or a woman who freely consents to work as a prostitute should have the right to do so. The point is merely that it is conceivable to have a right to the liberty to engage in almost any activity, but whether one really has a right to the liberty to engage in that kind of activity must be settled case by case.

The alternative would be to believe quite simply that the number of liberties ought to be maximized. This is an intelligible position, but I cannot think of any reason to hold it. In general, it is a safe bet that anyone who advocates the maximization of any one thing—liberties, pleasures, rationality, love, moderation, variety, virtue, or whatever—is unwise. Life's goods are too complex for any one of them to deserve such absolute priority, as far as I can see. There is a plurality of goods —and a plurality of rights that protect them.

So, on the one hand, the acknowledgment of economic rights does conflict with the liberty of other people to do as they like. But there is nothing necessarily special about this conflict. The simple fact that a supposed right would conflict with a liberty tells us only that it would indeed be a right: All rights function by imposing duties that restrict liberties. The right to physical security, or integrity of the person, conflicts with, and defeats, certain liberties. So do subsistence rights. Therefore, that some economic rights conflict with some liberties tells us nothing that we could not have deduced from the general nature of a right. Where the conflicts occur, we must decide how to settle them by comparing the specific economic right alleged with the specific right to liberty alleged. If the putative right of children in underdeveloped countries to adequate nutrition, for example, conflicts with the putative right of corporations to the liberty of choosing which crops to grow on which land, we must compare this particular right to nutrition and this particular right to liberty and decide, as a human community, which to acknowledge.

On the other hand, rights other than those to liberties enhance the value of those liberties to which there actually are rights. Certainly subsistence rights do not conflict with any liberty guaranteed as a right by the U.S. Constitution. And rights to every essential liberty, plus rights to economic security against the helplessness of starvation and exposure, are worth more, I submit, than rights to a few more inessential liberties—not basic liberties—at the price of vulnerability to economic forces that one cannot resist on one's own. Further, what duty-bearers lose in liberties, rights-bearers gain in the value of liberties; and, provided rights are equal, duty-bearers are themselves also rights-bearers. The liberties they lose as duty-bearers, all lose. The rights others gain against them, they too gain as rights-bearers against others.

This will become clearer as we look first at the general structure of a human right and then specifically at subsistence rights.

## Rights as Social Guarantees against Standard Threats

It can be useful to think of a human right as providing "(1) the rational basis for a justified demand (2) that the actual enjoyment of a substance be (3) socially guaranteed against standard threats."[6] "Substance" is merely a vague place-holder for whatever a right is a right to: freedom of the press, not being held in slavery, physical security, due process, adequate shelter, or whatever. Most relevant here is the third part of the characterization, which indicates that the general structure of a right includes two central elements: a threat and a guarantee, or protection, against that threat. The threats, human or natural, are there and real whether anyone recognizes them or not. The guarantee, or social protection, is there only if people decide to create it by constructing institutions and processes that will provide it.

The human rights we already enjoy are constituted by the rationally justified social guarantees we have already designed and constructed against the threats we have already recognized. The human rights we do not yet enjoy, but ought to enjoy, are the similar rationally justified guarantees against threats that already hang over us but are not yet clearly conceived or fully acknowledged. Human rights are enjoyed when social arrangements have been made on a rational basis so that we can work together to protect each other against recognized threats. New human rights evolve as we comprehend the seriousness and pervasiveness of previously ignored threats and we realize that guarantees or social arrangements against those threats could be made without sacrificing anything of greater value. This has been happening in recent years with subsistence rights.

Most controversies about which human rights should be acknowledged turn, then, around two points of debate: first, whether a particular threat is sufficiently serious and is otherwise appropriate to be the substance of a human right; and, second, whether the guarantees that would have to be built to protect people would not themselves create burdens or threats that would be worse than the threat they protect against—in other words, whether the cure would be worse than the disease. The possibility that the cure might be worse than the disease—that the potential new right might conflict with a critical old right—prevents us from immediately inferring a right wherever a

---

[6] Shue, *Basic Rights*, p. 13. A useful general analysis is James W. Nickel, "Are Human Rights Utopian?" *Philosophy & Public Affairs*, vol. 11, no. 3 (Summer 1982), pp. 246–64; see especially the summary table on p. 249. Since Nickel and I do agree on many points—in part because I have learned from him—and since we are now sometimes yoked as co-conspirators [see, for example, Tibor Machan, "Some Philosophical Aspects of National Labor Policy," *Harvard Journal of Law and Public Policy*, 4 (Summer 1981), p. 149, n. 205], it is perhaps only fair to Nickel to note in addition that he is not at all persuaded by some of my arguments (nor I by his alleged counterexamples). See James W. Nickel and Lizbeth L. Hasse, "Book Review," *California Law Review*, vol. 69, no. 5 (September 1981), pp. 1569–86.

serious threat exists. Not only must the threat itself pose a serious danger to a vital interest, but the social arrangements needed to guard against the threat must themselves not threaten other vital interests.

For example, Ernest W. Lefever, who is a reliable source of wild exaggerations on the subject of human rights, has recently asserted that economic and social rights "are really objectives and aspirations, not rights, because they cannot be guaranteed by any government unless it is totalitarian. The price of gaining these 'rights' is the sacrifice of freedom itself."[7] That some of the European social democracies are among the nations that have most fully guaranteed basic economic and social rights makes Lefever's specific claim that only totalitarian social institutions can guarantee these rights incredible. But the general form of the objection is perfectly appropriate: A good argument against a putative right would be an actual demonstration that, however serious the threat in question, the institutions that would enable people to guard each other against the threat would undermine other protections against other threats—here, protections against deprivations of liberty. I shall return later to less extreme arguments about whether institutions protecting subsistence are incompatible with institutions protecting liberty.

Including in the analysis of human rights these elements of threat and guarantee makes it easier to explain how making a mistake about a human right—having the wrong right—is possible. Any actual social consensus may include superfluous "rights" that ought not to be recognized but are; or it may omit urgent rights that ought to be included but are not. A right is superfluous when either the threat is not as serious as alleged or the burdens and duties created by the social provisions necessary to deal with the threat are more of a problem themselves than the original threat would have been; and, obviously, a critical right is missing when a threat is ignored or underestimated or when the burdens of cooperating to defend each other against that threat are exaggerated.

Noticing that rights are responses to threats also enables us to explain clearly how the list of human rights can legitimately, if only gradually, change over the centuries. The reasonableness of providing social guarantees against threats is always to be judged partly by assessing the seriousness of the threat against the availability of the human resources for dealing with the threat. The explanation of how the list of rights can change is simply that the kinds of threats against which human society can feasibly protect its members changes, both

---

[7] Ernest W. Lefever, "Human Rights and U.S. Foreign Policy: Security or Pax Sovietica," *Vital Speeches of the Day* (March 15, 1982), p. 343.

because threats themselves advance and recede and because the resources of society for dealing with threats advance and recede.

The fact that the best protection against serious threats is often a social institution must not obscure the other fact, with which it is perfectly compatible, that some of the worst threats to human rights are also social institutions, political and economic. As the defenders of civil and political rights never tire of repeating—correctly, as far as they go—it was social institutions, specifically oppressive governments, *against* which the earliest rights were asserted. The Magna Carta demanded that the (royal) government get off the (noble) people's backs. And never have rights been violated more seriously than by the regimes of Hitler and Stalin. All this is not merely true, it is extremely important.

What follows, however, is that good government rather than bad government is needed. What does not follow is that the best government is the least government. The best government is the government that most fully honors human rights. Sometimes honoring human rights means simply not violating rights, which is in itself a major achievement; but sometimes, too, it means protecting rights with institutions well designed for the job. Which of these institutions should be governmental is an open question.

## Reasons for Subsistence Rights

Why should there be rights to subsistence, and why are these rights so firmly entrenched in the international consensus about human rights? I do not suggest that subsistence rights are the most basic rights. Other rights, including those to physical security and political liberty, are equally basic.[8] I will, however, try to establish that subsistence rights are no less basic and no less genuine than any other rights, including civil and political rights.

The most fundamental rights are social guarantees for individuals against the threats to which they are otherwise most vulnerable: "Basic rights are a shield for the defenseless against at least some of the more devastating and more common of life's threats."[9] The vulnerability of human beings is the result of our physical fragility. It is extraordinarily easy to put a human being out of business by damaging the workings of his or her body. To make an analogy with war, the damage can be produced either by direct attack or by deprivation of vital supplies. A few minutes without breathable air, a few days without potable water,

---

[8] Shue, *Basic Rights*, chap. 3.
[9] Ibid., p. 18.

or a few weeks without edible food and the physical damage to a human being can be as severe, irreversible, and fatal as the damage from a bullet or a bomb.

Sometimes it is helpful to divide human vulnerability into physical security and economic security; I call the latter subsistence. Protecting physical security is then a matter of preventing torture, rape, "disappearance," beatings, and other direct physical assaults. Protecting economic security, or subsistence, is a matter of preventing the disruption of supplies of food, water, clothing, housing, and so forth, and the jobs that are ordinarily people's only means of obtaining the income needed to purchase those supplies.

But subsistence or economic security is only a half-step away from physical security. You need food for the same reason you need not to be beaten up: so that your body will keep working. The analogy with war is helpful. Cutting off food supplies to a garrison is an act of war just as much as bombing the garrison, even though the former is a deprivation of subsistence and the latter is a direct assault upon physical security. The blockade, if it is maintained with enough patience, sometimes works more surely than the bombing.

It is not at all unusual today for a government to "fight inflation" with economic policies that eliminate jobs, thereby depriving citizens of their only existing means of subsistence, and to provide no alternative means of subsistence. Such policies are a virtual government blockade against the unemployed whose jobs disappear as a result of the government's choice. It is also not unusual for a corporation to make a switch in technology that eliminates jobs or to transfer a plant out of an area in which alternative jobs and the capital to create them do not exist. Persons' diet, health, and even lives are vulnerable to devastation unless social guarantees exist for necessities like food. "Why don't they just plant a little vegetable garden?" presupposes, among other things, access to arable land. Anyone who has been outside the international hotel section of cities like Jakarta, Mexico City, Rio de Janeiro, and Calcutta knows what an unreachable paradise a little vegetable garden can seem. For that matter, one can only try to imagine more than a few people trying to grow their own food in Los Angeles or New York.

In fact, the line between physical security and economic security is difficult to maintain. Consider potable water. In an underdeveloped country, for example, the provision of unpolluted water may be a matter of installing proper sewage and taking other positive measures to remove pollutants like cholera organisms that are already in the water. This seems to be a matter of what some theorists like to call positive duties because various public health measures, which cost money, have to be undertaken in order to make improvements in the initial situation. In a wealthy industrialized country like the United States, however, we normally think of unpolluted water as a matter of so-called negative duties. Since the basic sewage facilities and many other public health measures were taken long ago, our initial condition is clean water. We do not need to clean up dirty water—we need to prevent the dirtying of clean water by industrial chemicals and other pollutants.

The point here is that whether a society has a negative duty to protect clean water against contaminating interference or a positive duty to clean up water that starts out as dirty is largely a matter of which stage in a continuous historical process one takes as the initial condition. The cholera organisms in the underdeveloped countries are the result of previous human activity (no doubt unsuspecting of the consequences) just as the PCBs in the industrialized countries are (again, in the beginning, all unsuspecting). Insofar as a guarantee of unpolluted water is conceived as a matter of positive public health measures, it seems better construed as the provision of economic security or subsistence. Insofar as a guarantee of unpolluted water is conceived as protecting currently potable sources against contamination, it seems best construed as the provision of physical security. One can ask whether introducing a carcinogen into one's water supply is not analogous to assaulting one's body. Indeed, is it not an actual case of assaulting one's body, like putting poison in one's cocktail?

My own view is that when the abstract distinction between physical security and subsistence is doing more to confuse matters than to keep them straight, as it is here, theorists should stop insisting upon that distinction and simply think in concrete terms of social guarantees, which will always involve some negative duties and some positive duties against serious, general, and remediable threats.[10] Insofar as it becomes difficult to distinguish sharply between basic rights to physical security and basic rights to subsistence, it becomes more implausible than ever to maintain that affluent people have a right to measures against carcinogens but poor people have no right to measures against cholera.

---

[10] For my central argument that all rights have both positive and negative duties, and that one therefore cannot usefully classify rights as positive rights or negative rights, see *Basic Rights*, chap. 2. For much further discussion of exactly how to formulate the duties correlative to the right to food, in particular, see Philip Alston and Katarina Tomasevski, eds., *The Right to Food* (Leiden: Martinus Nijhoff, forthcoming).

Subsistence rights have appropriately been widely recognized, then, because they constitute social guarantees against one of the most devastating forms of helplessness to which humanity is vulnerable: a form of helplessness that can prevent the enjoyment of any other right, not to mention the achievement of goals far more elevated than mere survival. A guarantee of subsistence for those who *cannot* provide it for themselves is a necessary condition for a genuine and meaningful guarantee of anything else, including the substances of other rights.

Let me try now to guard against two common misunderstandings. First, emphasizing subsistence items may appear to constitute some crass form of materialism: all that matters is making money and feeding one's face. What happened to human dignity and to religion, art, and culture, it might be asked. The sarcastic answer is that those preoccupied with human dignity should try maintaining theirs while walking the streets of a slum in rags desperately trying to think of a noncriminal activity that will bring in enough food for one more day. The real answer, however, is that nothing that I am saying about the equal primacy of subsistence rights with other basic rights, including physical security and political liberty, presupposes or implies any rankings among the higher things of life. Enjoying the guarantee of the freedom to write poetry is a nobler endeavor than enjoying the guarantee of shelter against the cold. Basic rights like subsistence come first precisely because they are the lowest—that is, the most fundamental—activities, not the highest.

The satisfaction of mere material wants for nonnecessities could not be defended as the substance of a right, not even of a nonbasic right. Basic rights defend the necessities that underlie both the inspirations and the mere preferences. "Starving poet" is itself a bit of poetic license: The world's malnourished millions do not produce a great number of poems. Many fundamental rights, like the right to physical security against torture, are merely protections against the worst—guarantees against vulnerabilities—provided so that those shielded can turn their own attention to higher things or to mere preferences, as they choose.

A second question can be asked: Is not the elimination of persons' livelihood or other means of access to food, shelter, and other subsistence items often the result of a natural disaster, not of a government or a corporate decision? This, however, is decreasingly true as modern economic and political institutions—market and nonmarket—increase in their power over what remains of "nature." Nothing is more oppressive than a market to which one has no access. This decline of the natural—and of the autonomous access of individuals to natural resources—is, in fact, a matter of monumental importance, and we need to confront it directly and fully.

## Driving Back the Natural

Why has it traditionally seemed so clear to North Atlantic theorists that everyone has a right not to be physically assaulted but has no right to the fulfillment of even so basic a need as the need for adequate nutrition? Why would the drafters of the U.S. Constitution probably have thought the suggestion of including subsistence rights bizarre? Both assault and malnutrition are physical harms—indeed harms that can be fatal. Why should it have been thought that we are entitled to the protection of a right against the one but not entitled to the protection constituted by a right in the case of the other? If the protections that are constitutionally guaranteed are as incomplete as they now seem, what caused the blindspot?

Many factors contributed, of course, including the unchallenged assumption of only "moderate scarcity"—that is, no genuine scarcity at all—that was always a premise of liberal theory. And the assumption seemed confirmed by the abundance and the open frontier of the New World. One other fundamental idea seems to have been that we are entitled to protection as a right only against harms that are inflicted by other people.[11] We need to explore this idea briefly, and I will use the term "social threats" to describe the source of harms that are caused by the actions of other people. Thus an assault is a very clear result of a social threat, since the source of the harm is the action of another human being. People were not considered by mainstream North Atlantic thought to have a right to protection against malnutrition because malnutrition was viewed to be a natural rather than a

---

[11] Naturally this can be only an extremely incomplete suggestion of the sources of the imbalance. Civil and political rights are standardly said to have a number of distinguishing features that (1) demarcate them sharply from economic, social, and cultural rights and (2) provide the basis for assigning priority to the civil and political ones. For insightful critiques of the arguments for thinking that the distinguishing features are reasons for an assignment of priority, see Charles R. Beitz, "Human Rights and Social Justice," in Peter G. Brown and Douglas MacLean, eds., *Human Rights and U.S. Foreign Policy* (Lexington, Mass.: Lexington Books, 1979), pp. 45–63, esp. 45–53. For a critique of the thesis that the two groups of rights are sharply distinguishable, see Henry Shue, *Basic Rights*, chap. 2.

One of the most sophisticated formulations and defenses of a highly plausible version of what he calls the "priority of liberty" is in John Rawls, *A Theory of Justice* (Cambridge, Mass.: Belknap Press, 1971). A decisive refutation of the Rawlsian scheme is in Norman Daniels, "Equal Liberty and Unequal Worth of Liberty," in Norman Daniels, ed., *Reading Rawls: Critical Studies of A Theory of Justice* (New York: Basic Books, 1974), pp. 253–81.

social threat. I use the term "natural threat" to refer to the source of harms primarily caused by nonhuman factors—what we may roughly call nature. Insofar as malnutrition is caused by, say, flood or drought, it is the result of a natural threat. And if people may have rights to protection only against social threats, not natural threats, then they clearly are not entitled to protection against inadequate nutrition due to the effects of drought or flood.

Although I think it is fairly clear that the crucial line was the often implicit one between social threat and natural threat, it is considerably more difficult to say why this line rather than any other was used as the boundary between what could be guaranteed as a right and what could not be guaranteed as a right. Two complementary explanations are apparent. First, many thinkers in Europe and the United States have treated society as a largely artificial creation, as if it were, for example, the product of a social contract or an act of consent among persons who had previously lived in a state of nature. This rather implausible view that society is somehow unnatural, or helpfully viewed as if it were unnatural, and that human beings could have pre-dated human society, encourages the following thought. If having moved from a natural state to a social state through an act of voluntary consent is to be considered rational, then we must be at least no worse off in society than we were prior to society. This requirement suggests that within society we should be protected against the harms that close association makes more likely, and these are precisely social threats. If our fancied voluntary formation of society has brought us into closer contact with each other than was natural or inevitable, then we are at least to be protected against the kinds of harms that we can newly inflict upon each other. These are social threats, and so our rights are entitlements to protection against social threats. Although the preoccupation of many North Atlantic thinkers with the notion of a voluntary social contract helps to explain historically the infatuation with the distinction between social threats and natural threats, it does little to justify this distinction, especially to the extent that one sees the implausibility of the notion that society—governments are a different kettle of fish—is indeed somehow artificial.

A second source of the importance attached to the line between social threat and natural threat may have been the Rousseauean notion that social threats are worse than natural threats because social threats arise from conscious human intentions. That the harms they produce are inflicted knowingly and even intentionally by other people may seem to mean that they add insult to injury. When one suffers a social harm, one is not only made worse off but made worse off because someone else wished it to be so. Rights that are constituted by protection against the harmful intentions of others may therefore seem especially important because they protect us not simply against harmful effects but against evil intentions, not merely against misfortune but against malevolence.

Whatever the intellectual sources of the primacy of protection against social threats rather than protection against natural threats, what has now happened is not so much that we have come to doubt that social concern with social threat should be paramount over concern with natural threat, as that the location of the line between the social and the natural has shifted sharply. Much less is now natural than used to be. Social control, through expanded government, especially increased government management of the economy in both so-called capitalist societies and so-called socialist societies, and through improved science and technology, has been extended over much that used to be natural and outside the realm of human manipulation and control. As we have driven back the boundaries of the natural we have extended not only human control but, I am suggesting, human responsibility.

The thesis that we are collectively responsible for the effects of the institutions that we collectively control is a substantial moral thesis that requires explicit defense. It is, however, a far more modest account of social responsibility than, for example, the one implicit in Burke's notion of society as

> a partnership in all art; a partnership in every virtue and in all perfection. As the ends of such a partnership cannot be obtained in many generations, it becomes a partnership between those who are living, those who are dead, and those who are to be born.[12]

I am suggesting here only that one bears some responsibility for some physical harm at least in proportion to one's control over or influence upon the social institutions—governments, corporations, unions, armies, churches, newspapers—that inflict that harm upon other people. How much influence one has over a particular institution is a factual matter.

The harm need not have been intended; the contrary assumption is part of what is wrong with the Rousseauean thesis that it is the evil eye focused upon the victim that makes the damage so much more

---

[12] Edmund Burke, *The Works of the Right Honorable Edmund Burke*, 3d ed. (Boston: Little, Brown, and Co., 1869), vol. 3, p. 359.

terrible.[13] I am responsible for some of the effects I have upon other people. The effects for which I am responsible are not restricted to effects I intended to have or to effects I produced all by myself. I also bear some (not all) of the responsibility for some (not all) of the jointly produced, unintended effects of how I live my life, including the institutions I support and am supported by politically, economically, and intellectually. Some, not all—which? I return to the formulation of one principle for allocating responsibility after a concrete illustration.

Consider the example of the basic need for food. My point is not that people have become less vulnerable to natural forces, but that they have become very much more vulnerable to social forces, especially national and international government economic activity and transnational corporate activity, in addition to natural forces. One way by which to be entitled to food is to grow it yourself and own it; the "and own it" is important, of course, because in many kinds of arrangements (like share-cropping) the producer does not own all he produces. How much one owns even of what one produces through one's own labor is determined by the legal system and customary social relations. Naturally if one does not grow and own adequate food, then one must exchange something one does own, either one's labor or some commodity or piece of property, for food. Which things one owns is determined by the legal system, and the prices that can be obtained for labor are conditioned by the economic system, including government policies for fighting inflation, for encouraging foreign investment, and so forth.[14]

My point here is not that any particular legal or economic system is good, bad, or indifferent. The point is that the individual with his or her basic needs is embedded in a complex system of legal, economic, and political institutions—a complex social system. The romantic conception of the individual struggling against nature to satisfy basic needs could hardly be further from the truth. But the traditional sharp dichotomy between genuine rights and basic economic needs that are taken to be important but not to be the subjects of rights depends upon accepting this grossly inaccurate picture as accurate. For the dichotomy depends upon the notion that failures in the fulfillment of basic needs, such as famines, are natural harms fully explicable by

---

[13] See John Charvet, *The Social Problem in the Philosophy of Rousseau* (New York: Cambridge University Press, 1974).

[14] For a penetrating economic analysis of the causes of famine, see Amartya Sen, *Poverty and Famines: An Essay on Entitlement and Deprivation* (Oxford: Clarendon Press, 1981).

factors like floods and droughts, and not social harms, largely explicable by the action of other people and the economic and political policies of governments. But in the case of malnutrition, just as in the case of bodily assault, it is other people who are both the worst threat and the best protection against physical harm. Their worst and their best is done through social institutions: police who protect the weak and police who torture the innocent, agribusinesses that improve techniques and agribusinesses that divert land.

It is, therefore, perfectly reasonable that people should have rights to protection against social threats like malnutrition, just as they have rights to protection against social threats like bodily assault. In other words, it is perfectly reasonable that people should have rights to assistance in the fulfillment of their basic needs, if economic and political policies have left them unable to do so themselves. And this means that our responsibilities to deal, for example, with malnutrition are not what used to be called duties of benevolence or humanitarian matters. They are duties to fulfill rights—the most basic duties of all.

What is difficult—and it is very difficult—is to specify *which* of the jointly or socially produced, unintended effects any given individual bears responsibility for. (This includes the question of which beneficial effects I am entitled to take credit for, as well as the question of which harmful effects I must bear the blame for, although I am ignoring this brighter side here.) Specification of sensible, well-informed principles for the allocation of responsibility is, I think, one of the central tasks of contemporary political philosophy.[15] I have elsewhere suggested—somewhat misleadingly—that we sometimes bear "responsibility through complicity—complicity by continuing acceptance of benefits."[16] The qualification "continuing" is a reference to information: continuing to accept the benefits of an institution after learning about the severe harms caused by that institution.

Responsibility through (informed) complicity replaces Rousseau's *intended* harms with *willingly accepted* harms. One may not have intended to cause anyone any harm at all, but once one knows that serious physical harm is resulting from the ongoing operation of some institution the benefits of which one continues to accept, one can no longer claim to be unwilling for the harm to be done: "In such situa-

---

[15] It is the failure to go beyond the insistence that there must be limits on responsibility and to tackle the specification of some of the needed limits that makes disappointing James S. Fishkin's *The Limits of Obligation* (New Haven: Yale University Press, 1982).

[16] Henry Shue, "Exporting Hazards," in Peter G. Brown and Henry Shue, eds., *Boundaries: National Autonomy and Its Limits*, Maryland Studies in Public Philosophy (Totowa, N.J.: Rowman and Allanheld, 1981), p. 136.

tions, knowledge is not only power but also responsibility, because it places us in a position to act."[17] We may initially have intended no harm, but we cannot maintain that we are unwilling for the harm to continue once we know that an institution upon which we have some influence is causing the harm and we do nothing to eliminate the harmful effects.

What may be misleading about the preceding is any suggestion that responsibility falls upon someone only if the person happens to blunder across what amounts to some incriminating evidence about one of the social institutions that the person benefits from or supports. This would make degrees of responsibility contingent upon happenstance affecting which information one chanced across. Thus, if my government were engaged in all sorts of mischief in Honduras but I did not know (or care to know) about it, I would have no responsibility for it. If my callous treatment is pushing my secretary toward a nervous breakdown but I have not noticed, then it would be her problem, not mine.

This is not what we think. On the contrary, we hold people responsible—to some degree, in some cases—for the harms to which they contribute not only unintentionally but even unknowingly. This is what "callous" means: You did not need to will the harm because you were too insensitive to the needs of others to notice that you were harming them. We do sometimes condemn individuals and institutions for having failed to foresee and prevent serious harms. We hold them responsible for having failed, in short, to take due care. We have a *responsibility to take due care.*

No one thinks that the manufacturers of Thalidomide intended to cause infants to be limbless, or even, as far as I know, that they willingly acquiesced after they had the information incriminating their drug. But people generally still held them responsible, because it is the business of drug firms to find out the side-effects of new compounds. We held them responsible for not taking due care. If an obstetrician drops a baby and fractures its skull, we do not assume the act was intentional and charge him or her with murder. But we still hold the obstetrician responsible for not having taken due care—it is the business of obstetricians to handle babies without causing them harm.

Not everyone is as vulnerable as an infant, although it is well worth remembering that most of the people in the world's population now—not to mention most of the malnourished and most of the refugees—are children. And most causal relations are far less linear and simple than the mother's taking Thalidomide and the offspring's

---

[17] Ibid.

lacking arms or legs. But we do still believe that large and complex institutions and organizations like governments, corporations, armies, and unions ought to include in their plans mechanisms for taking due care. One of the functions that some part of the organization should perform is to expect what would otherwise be unexpected harms and head them off. Not to do so is a failure in intelligence, in both senses of "intelligence."

Indeed, the failure to take due care is as much what the Greeks would have called an intellectual vice as it is a moral vice in the narrower modern sense. If a post-Kantian moral vice consists of intending or willing evil, and an intellectual vice is a failure to see or to understand which actions are good and which are evil, then the failure to take due care may at least as often be a failure to foresee a harm as a willful failure to prevent it once foreseen. It is easier to think in terms of the moral failings of individuals than in terms of the intellectual failings of institutions. It is also anachronistic in this age of bureaucratic planning, public and private.

### The Transnational Duty to Build Adequate Institutions

Most of the people in circumstances in which they must (and may) invoke their subsistence rights—circumstances in which they cannot provide for their own subsistence—are outside the United States. Almost surely most are, in fact, also children. Many of the duties correlative to their subsistence rights fall upon their own better-off compatriots; but some of these subsistence duties, as they may be called, fall upon affluent foreigners, including affluent residents of the United States. Some of the duties are, then, what would traditionally have been called universal duties and what we might now more naturally call transnational duties.

We obviously lack at present adequate institutions for the performance of the more positive of these transnational responsibilities, although treaties like the International Covenant on Economic, Social and Cultural Rights and organizations like the International Labor Organization and the World Health Organization are important institutional beginnings. The inadequacies of traditional government-to-government foreign aid, as well as the failings of intergovernmental organizations like the World Bank, are well known and much analyzed. Insofar as nongovernmental transfers are taken to be "humanitarian" (in the sense of discretionary), we fail to signify that what are being fulfilled are indeed people's rights. Indisputably we are on an institutional frontier, and most of our efforts are fairly primitive.

93

Soon, however, the argument is liable to take the following general form, which is perverse: Of course the prompt fulfillment of subsistence rights would be a fine thing; but the available institutions, national or international, are simply not now adequate to the task, so we will not be able to do very much better for a while—although we will certainly try our best, given the institutions with which we have to work. This argument is analogous to the residents on a rough and lawless frontier saying: "Gee, wouldn't it be nice if we had a sheriff with the authority to form a posse and round up outlaws, but since we don't have any institutions of law and order here, I guess the best we can do is to let everyone fight for himself."

Building an adequate institution where there is none is admittedly a difficult undertaking, even when the institution in question is so rudimentary as some minimal law enforcement. The transition from no institution to an institution is made especially difficult because of the obvious challenge of motivating people to make the transition. Even if having the institution would be in everyone's interest, it is usually not in anyone's interest to act as if the institution is already in place before it actually is. It may be in my own interest that laws should be enforced, even against me as well as against other people, but it is not in my interest simply to obey model laws while others can get away with ignoring them. To obey the law becomes in my interest only at the time when the law becomes enforceable. The challenge is making any law enforceable when people do not yet have any interest in obeying it. If the building of rudimentary institutions of law and order on a frontier is this complex, one can easily imagine the difficulty with instituting new economic and social institutions to enable people to enjoy their subsistence rights. The problem is, however, no different in principle.

If you think that people have a right not to be shot down in the street, you do not say fatalistically that if we had a sheriff, we could deal with this problem, but since we lack the relevant institution we will just have to keep struggling along. "To will the end is to will the means," as Kant observed. In other words, if we really ought to accomplish some goals, then we really ought to take the necessary steps to get there. And if taking the necessary steps means building some institution that may be long and hard in coming, then we ought to get started. What we ought not to do is to use the absence of the institutions as an excuse for failing to accomplish the purpose.

This is why I have called the excuse of inadequate institutions not simply misguided but perverse. The absence of the means for fulfilling a goal is being used as the excuse for not fulfilling it, when, if we seriously had the goal, we would be working on the creation of the necessary bridges from here to there.

That people do actually have a right to something like adequate food does not mean merely that we should assist them in obtaining adequate food if doing so is easy and convenient. It means that we have a duty, correlative to their right, to do what must be done for them to enjoy their right. It is perfectly possible, as in the case of the frontier town without a sheriff, that before we can fulfill a right we must change existing institutions or build new ones. If so, then the energetic and imaginative building of the institutions that will fulfill the right is our first duty in response to that right. The framers of the U.S. Constitution need not have been the last American pioneers in the realm of rights.

### Recent Implementation and the Ideological Temptation

Most of the people whose subsistence rights are not being fulfilled today live outside the United States. Thus, it is U.S. foreign policy that has the greatest potential for increasing the enjoyment of subsistence rights. Sadly the Reagan administration sank below the level of the Carter administration, which in its foreign policy at least acknowledged subsistence rights in principle while largely ignoring them in practice.[18]

The final *Country Reports on Human Rights Practices* prepared by the Carter administration in 1980 accurately observed:

> Internationally-recognized rights can be grouped into three broad categories: first, the right to be free from government violations of the integrity of the person—violations such as torture . . . ; second, the right to the fulfillment of vital needs such as food, shelter, health care and education; and third, the right to enjoy civil and political liberties.[19]

---

[18] For some of my criticisms of the Carter policy on human rights while it was in force, see *Basic Rights*, pp. 5–9, 155–74.

[19] U.S. Congress, Senate, Committee on Foreign Relations, and House, Committee on Foreign Affairs, *Country Reports on Human Rights Practices*, 97th Congress, 1st session, February 2, 1981, p. 2.

Thoughtful readers will have noticed that the tripartite division of rights into integrity of the person, fulfillment of vital needs, and enjoyment of civil and political liberties does not easily map onto the dichotomy of civil/political and economic/social/cultural. Both these categorizations are too gross to be much help, but the tripartite division is the more accurate reflection of practice. Both ignore the distinction between basic and nonbasic rights, which, although also crude, cuts across them both to make one useful point. The division of rights into first, second, and third generations—in this essay I am entirely leaving aside putative third-generation rights—is yet another cut. Some theorist needs to sort all this out comprehensively.

In the first *Country Reports on Human Rights Practices* completed under the Reagan administration during 1981 only the first category (integrity of the person) and the third category (civil and political liberties) make an appearance—the second category has simply evaporated. In 1981, with one stroke of the bureaucratic pen, economic rights—subsistence rights and all—were suddenly made to disappear from U.S. foreign policy. Far from helping to construct adequate institutions to implement subsistence rights, the Human Rights Bureau of the U.S. State Department under the Reagan administration explicitly rejected *in toto* the second of the three general categories of internationally recognized human rights that were correctly acknowledged throughout the Carter administration beginning with the fundamental policy address in April 1977 by Secretary of State Cyrus Vance.[20] The new State Department had somehow waved away all the rights in the International Covenant on Economic, Social and Cultural Rights, even the most basic ones.

This conscious omission was given one explicit rationale in the 1981 *Country Reports*, a rationale that was reprinted for emphasis in the *State Department Bulletin*. The following was offered as the justification for the abrupt disappearance of economic rights:

> The urgency and moral seriousness of the need to eliminate starvation and poverty from the world are unquestionable, and continue to motivate large American foreign aid efforts. However, the idea of economic and social rights is easily abused by repressive governments which claim that they promote human rights even though they deny their citizens the basic rights to the integrity of the person, as well as civil and political rights. This justification for repression has in fact been extensively used. No category of rights should be allowed to become an excuse for the denial of other rights. For this reason, the term economic and social rights is, for the most part, not used in this year's Reports. A section on Economic and Social Circumstances is included because of the moral imperative of conquering poverty and since an under-

---

[20] Secretary of State Cyrus R. Vance, "Human Rights Policy," April 30, 1977 (Washington, D.C.: Office of Media Services, Bureau of Public Affairs, Department of State), PR 194, p. 1. The inclusion of "the right to the fulfillment of such vital needs as food, shelter, health care, and education" was reaffirmed by Deputy Secretary of State Warren Christopher in "Human Rights: Principle and Realism," August 9, 1977 (Washington: Office of Media Services, Bureau of Public Affairs, Department of State), PR 374, p. 1.

No nostalgia for the Carter administration's handling of economic rights is invoked. I am simply noting that its official statements accurately reflected the international law of human rights. Rhetoric is rhetoric, but official rhetoric sometimes matters.

standing of these circumstances is useful in appreciating the conditions under which the struggle for political and civil liberties is carried on in a particular country.[21]

This is a very poor argument. Its premise is true: dictators often eliminate freedom in the name of bread, which they usually also fail to provide; this was precisely the excuse given in 1972 by President Marcos of the Philippines when he introduced a decade of martial law in the name of land reform.[22] But we cannot abandon rights simply because dictators abuse their names. And the abuse works in both directions: People are also subjected to malnutrition in the name of preserving freedom, as in Chile under Pinochet. Further, there is little reason to suppose that wholesale trade-offs between civil rights and economic rights must, or even can, be made in either direction.[23]

Indeed, the above is such an implausible argument that to believe that people at the Department of State were motivated by it is difficult, and it seems more likely to have been an ad hoc rationale concocted for public consumption. This hypothesis is given support by the revelation of alternative official reasoning to the same conclusion. This reasoning emerges in the publicly accessible portions of the important but still largely classified policy memo that appears to have helped to prevent an assault upon the existence of the Bureau of Human Rights by the White House (in its frustration over the rejection by the Senate in June 1981 of its first nominee for assistant secretary of state for human rights and humanitarian affairs). This major memo was adopted by the Department of State on October 27, 1981, and partially released in connection with the second (successful) nomination of an assistant secretary of state for human rights. As quoted in the *New York Times* for November 5, 1981, that formal memo contained the following statements:

> "Human rights"—meaning political rights and civil liberties —conveys what is ultimately at issue in a contest with the Soviet bloc. The fundamental distinction is our respective attitudes toward freedom. . . . We should move away from

---

[21] "Country Reports on Human Rights Practices," *Department of State Bulletin*, vol. 82, no. 2061 (April 1982), p. 74.

[22] See Richard P. Claude, "Human Rights in the Philippines and U.S. Responsibility," in Peter G. Brown and Douglas MacLean, eds., *Human Rights and U.S. Foreign Policy* (Lexington, Mass.: Lexington Books, 1979), pp. 244–45.

[23] For a searching critique of the necessity and the possibility of the trade-offs, see Charles R. Beitz, "Democracy in Developing Societies," in Peter G. Brown and Henry Shue, eds., *Boundaries: National Autonomy and Its Limits*, Maryland Studies in Public Philosophy (Totowa, N.J.: Rowman and Allanheld, 1981), pp. 177–208.

"human rights" as a term, and begin to speak of "individual rights," "political rights" and "civil liberties."[24]

What this official policy statement, only selectively made public in 1981, was saying was the following: We want to emphasize the human rights that distinguish the United States from the Soviet Union. Those distinguishing rights are the civil and political ones. Therefore, if we should say "human rights," we would mean only civil and political rights—we do not include economic and social rights. If this reasoning saved the position of assistant secretary for human rights from political assault in 1981 only to possess the soul of the position for the indefinite future, any victory may have been pyrrhic indeed, especially because Congress would surely have turned back any attack on a position that is one of the bipartisan Congressional achievements of the previous decade.

The fundamental and fatal fault in this attempt to be politically clever by selling human rights to its enemies within the administration in anti-Soviet packaging is its intellectual barrenness. It makes no sense to try to pick and choose kinds of rights as if philosophical traditions and multilateral treaties were fruit stands from which one can pluck whatever suits one's current fancy and leave the rest to rot. Genuine rights have a rational basis, and spurious rights lack a rational basis. However important the "contest" with the Soviet bloc, the acknowledgment of human rights cannot responsibly be manipulated exclusively to score propaganda points.

An administration with a decent respect for the opinions of mankind would not have thought that it might simply follow its own preferences in human rights. Further, when U.S. statutes speak of "internationally recognized human rights," as do, for example, sections 116 and 502B of the Foreign Assistance Act, which are the statutory centerpieces of U.S. foreign policy concerning human rights, this is not empty rhetoric; this is an intentional reference by Congress to the consensus of humanity as clearly expressed in many forms in many places at many times. If any administration believes either that economic rights are not part of the existing consensus, or are but should not be part, it owes the rest of the international community concerned with human rights more than a one-paragraph explanation. That explanation should show why abandoning all economic rights, the basic and the nonbasic alike, is intellectually responsible, not merely politically convenient.

To use human rights in this fashion as a means toward cold war

---

[24] See "Excerpts from State Department Memo on Human Rights," *New York Times*, November 5, 1981.

goals poses a perennial and serious practical problem. A general difficulty with using one thing as a means to a second thing is that what is being used as the means will be emphasized when it seems to promote the goal and de-emphasized or ignored when it seems not to promote the goal. At the level of the means, one may well be very inconsistent since the means is after all to be employed only insofar as and when it promotes the goal. Thus the Reagan administration criticized the Polish dictators for imposing their martial law, as indeed they should have been criticized, presumably because criticisms of the Polish puppets could indeed effectively be used to embarrass the Soviet Union. But the administration was silent about the brutality of the latest Turkish dictatorship in the series that have punctuated Turkey's fitful efforts at democracy, presumably because the Turks are *our* brutes, not *their* brutes.[25] To criticize this inconsistency is not merely to pursue consistency for its own sake, nor is inconsistency itself the main problem.

Consistency about standards is a test of sincerity. If an administration says that it condemns martial law in Poland, not only because it likes to embarrass Communist regimes but also because we really are opposed to martial law itself, but then allows the U.S. secretary of defense to go to Turkey and praise the most recent imposition of martial law there, after our having lived happily with a decade of martial law in the Philippines (like Turkey, a dictatorship that is a military ally), it begins to appear that we are not actually opposed in principle to martial law but merely glad to use any excuse to criticize our adversaries.[26] Naturally, if martial law can sometimes be justified, it could be that the Turkish martial law was of some justified kind and the Polish martial law was of an unjustified kind. But when labor leaders in Turkey were being not only imprisoned, as in Poland, but executed, the distinctions that favored Turkish martial law were not readily apparent.[27] If significant distinctions could really have been drawn, then someone needed to draw them and dissolve the apparent inconsistency.

The doubts about sincerity that are otherwise raised by an inconsistency like this one are of general importance because it is especially

---

[25] "Unions in Turkey Face Harsh Repression," *Amnesty Action* (January 1982), p. 3. *Amnesty Action* is an official publication of Amnesty International USA. In spite of its history of lapsing into cruel dictatorship, Turkey is often described as part of the "Free World" because its troops are committed to NATO.

[26] "Weinberger Lauds Turk on Law, Order Efforts: As Europe Protests," *Washington Post*, December 6, 1981.

[27] *Amnesty Action* gives the names of national union leaders executed without trial since the current regime of martial law was imposed.

difficult to promote respect for human rights by governments that are your adversaries in the best of circumstances.[28] And if adversary governments become convinced that you care not about human rights violations but only about the propaganda value of discussing them, they are unlikely to respond to criticisms by improving attention to the rights. This creates a considerable and persistent danger of failing to help the victims of human rights violations by adversary governments. To criticize one's enemies only is to criticize them in a way that is guaranteed to have no effect. We betray the victims of those governments that we oppose precisely because of the severity of their violations of human rights when we criticize those violations in self-defeating ways.

In addition, using criticism of human rights violations only or even primarily as a means for embarrassing our enemies reinforces the always strong tendency to neglect speaking out against violations by governments that we do not want to embarrass, and we will thereby also betray the victims of human rights violations by our allies. Here we have a formula for betraying both the victims of our adversaries and the victims of our allies. Indefensible in principle and self-defeating in practice, U.S. foreign policy in the early 1980s was an embarrassment to the American heritage of defending the rights of those unable to defend themselves. Genuine subsistence rights were betrayed in the pursuit of illusory ideological gains.

---

[28] I have previously noted the difficulty of actually helping the victims of violations of human rights in the USSR while indulging the violations of anti-Communist allied governments. See Henry Shue, "Effective Support for Human Rights," in U.S. Congress, Senate, Committee on Foreign Relations, *Perceptions: Relations between the United States and the Soviet Union*, 95th Congress, 2d session (Washington, D.C.: Government Printing Office, 1978), pp. 410–13.

# 6

# American Constitutionalism
# and Individual Rights

NATHAN TARCOV

Americans disagree about how our rights are best protected—through the Bill of Rights itself, through activist constitutional adjudication, through the separation of powers, through an energetic federal government, through the states, through popular control and participation, or through a pluralist socioeconomic structure. But we tend to agree in speaking of the goal of our Constitution as securing rights. We even tend to agree in taking for granted the meaning and propriety of that goal.

Our language of securing rights is so attractive that it is increasingly spoken even by those who mean to justify forms of government entirely antithetical to American constitutionalism. We are therefore practically compelled to clarify the distinctive meaning of securing rights in our constitutional tradition and to contrast it with alternative understandings of the goal of a constitution. We must also recognize that securing rights does not exhaust even our own conception of the goals of a constitution.

## Political, Private, and Procedural Rights

There is a variety of rights that the Constitution is expressly concerned with securing. Some rights are essential to republican government itself. They are intrinsic to popular participation in politics, or more precisely, to popular control over a government exercised by the people not directly but only through their representatives. These rights include freedom of speech and the press, of assembly and petition,

The author wishes to acknowledge that this essay has benefited from David Greenstone's criticisms of an earlier draft.

perhaps also the right to bear arms, and of course election (at first directly only to the House of Representatives and indirectly to the Senate and the presidency).

A second kind of rights constitutes the private sphere and protects it from the political: the free exercise of religion; any non-political aspects of freedom of speech and of the press; the right to be secure in one's person, house, papers, and effects against unreasonable search or seizure; the right to make contracts whose obligation cannot be impaired; and the right to own private property subject to being taken for public use only with just compensation. The private sphere includes the life of the mind, the household or family, and the economy. The triad of the most fundamental private rights—those civil society exists to secure, according to Locke, namely life, liberty, and property—appear together in the Constitution only in that one cannot be deprived of them without due process of law. This fact illustrates most clearly the relation between the natural rights civil society is founded on and the civil rights it secures. Civil society exists to protect life, liberty, and property, but it does so precisely by wielding the power to deprive its members of life, liberty, and property. Those rights are more secure in civil society than in a state of nature, which is also to say they are more secure in a properly organized civil society than in a defective one, because they can be lost only in accordance with due process of law.

Due process is the hallmark of a third category, the procedural rights pertaining to trials (indictment by a grand jury, speedy and public trial by a local jury, immunity from double jeopardy and self-incrimination, and so on). All these procedural rights reflect the right to the rule of law implicit in the very granting of legislative, executive, and judicial powers in Articles I, II, and III. Americans have the constitutional right to be subject to no authority other than the legislated, executed, and judicially enforced law. The privilege of habeas corpus and the protection against ex post facto laws and bills of attainder are direct corollaries of the rule of law, which means that one can be deprived of life, liberty, or property only for an act one has committed against the law, not for an act that was legal at the time or was committed by someone else.

The Constitution protects a private sphere of civil rights, less extensive but more secure than natural liberty, partly directly and partly through the rights of political participation and through procedural rights. Although it is fair to assume that the procedural rights are only instrumental to the protection of life, liberty, and property, the rights of political participation or control may be understood either merely as fences erected to protect those private rights or as themselves rights of equal intrinsic value.

## The Rights of Individuals and of the People

If we are to distinguish the whole range of rights secured by the U.S. Constitution from alternative constitutional goals, including those that also speak of rights, the first distinction we should make is that the Constitution is founded on a conception of the rights of individuals rather than of humanity as a whole, or of the nation as such, or of races, classes, or other groups. Yet it is also emphatically an expression of the rights of "the people."

The Constitution, though ratified by states and established "between" those states, proclaims itself an act of "the People of the United States." As such it is an exercise of "the right of the people to alter or to abolish" any form of government "and to institute new government" proclaimed in the Declaration of Independence (as is almost candidly admitted in *The Federalist*).[1] The Declaration opens as a justification of *a people's* assuming that separate and equal station to which they have a natural right. But it founds that right of a people on the inalienable rights of "all men," that is to say, *of every individual,* to life, liberty, and the pursuit of happiness. It is to secure those rights of equally created individuals that governments are instituted. It is because of those individual rights that peoples have the collective right to institute governments. The right to alter or to abolish any form of government and to institute new governments on such principles and in such form as seem most likely to effect their safety and happiness is not the only collective right of the people, according to the Declaration. They also have "the right of representation in the legislature, a right inestimable to them." Their representatives in turn properly oppose invasions of "the rights of the people." In the absence of such representative legislatures, "the people at large" themselves have the right to exercise the legislative powers.

The acts complained of in the Declaration imply the existence of other rights of which they are the violations. Some of the acts are "abuses" of rightful power; others are "usurpations" of power without right. The Declaration complains, for example, that George III vetoed laws "most wholesome and necessary for the public good"

---

[1] Alexander Hamilton, James Madison, and John Jay, *The Federalist Papers,* ed. Clinton Rossiter (New York: New American Library, 1961), No. 40, p. 253; see also *Federalist* No. 78, p. 469.

but does not treat the veto power as illegitimate, as it does parliamentary "pretended legislation." Other acts, such as keeping standing armies in time of peace and imposing taxes, are complained of not as being wrongful in themselves but as having been done "without our consent." (This fact lends support to the argument in *Federalist* No. 23 through No. 36 for giving those powers to the legitimate and well-constructed government of the Constitution.)

All these injuries are violations of rights, whether of individual rights or of collective rights of the people to be governed in certain ways. The violated rights to an independent judiciary or to civil control over the military clearly belong to the people collectively. Either a whole society enjoys them or it does not, although when they are violated specific individuals surely suffer. Other injuries complained of attack the inalienable rights of individuals directly: most notably death and destruction in warfare and forcing men to kill or be killed in bearing arms against their fellow citizens. Other injuries listed attack those fundamental rights indirectly by striking at their procedural safeguards: depriving people of trial by jury, transporting them overseas for trial, and protecting their murderers by mock trials. (Due process should secure our rights not only by defending us from undeserved punishment but also by punishing those who deprive us of our rights.) Although the objection to taxation is explicitly to its imposition without consent, it is not clear whether quartering troops and cutting off trade are wrongful only because done by an unacknowledged parliament. (Although the Third Amendment to the Constitution would settle that troops could be quartered in war "in a manner to be prescribed by law," the author of the Declaration, as president, would have to assert the constitutionality of his embargo without explicit textual warrant.)[2]

Some injuries violate immediately or ultimately both the collective rights of the people and the rights of individuals, which are distinct in theory but closely connected in practice. Taxation without representation violates not only the individual's right to property but also the people's collective right to consent. For when the Declaration complains of imposing taxes without "our consent," it means the same thing as when it complains of keeping standing armies without "the consent of our legislatures." John Locke had written that gov-

---

[2] In "A Summary View of the Rights of British America," Jefferson stated that "the exercise of a free trade with all parts of the world" was "possessed by the American colonists as of natural right." But he immediately added that "no law of their own had taken away or abridged" it, implying that a legislature enjoying consent could do so. Thomas Jefferson, *The Portable Thomas Jefferson*, ed. Merrill D. Peterson (New York: Viking Press, 1975), p. 6.

ernment *"cannot take* from any Man any part of his *Property* without his own consent" but had glossed "his own consent" as "*i.e.*, the Consent of the Majority, giving it either by themselves, or their Representatives chosen by them."[3] Locke also explained, of the right to representation generally, that the people have reserved "to themselves the Choice of their *Representatives*, as the Fence to their *Properties*."[4] The collective rights of the people, of which the Constitution is itself an expression as well as a compendium, secure the rights of individuals.

## What Constitutes a People?

It is difficult to be sure what constitutes that crucial collectivity the Declaration calls a people, which establishes the Constitution and exercises rights that, in turn, secure the rights of individuals. The first sentence of the Declaration seems to suggest that "one people" is already "one people" somehow distinct from "another" even when both are still joined by "political bands." This distinction of peoples exists despite "the ties of our common kindred" and "consanguinity," which Americans had invoked in their previous appeals to their "British brethren." (A passage of Jefferson's, omitted by Congress, makes clear that "our common blood" is not British but specifically English as opposed to "Scotch.")[5] Neither political independence nor common descent seems to be what constitutes a people.

Congress did not clarify what, other than common descent or political independence, constitutes "one people." Jefferson's draft, however, suggests that the Americans and the British might have been "a free and great people together." It seems almost as if they had been one people bound by "love" and "affection," however "agonizing," until the British proved "unfeeling brethren"—a line of argument highlighted in Garry Wills's interpretation of Jefferson's Declaration as a document of Scottish sentimental moral theory.[6] But we should not make too much of this sentimental appeal, let alone infer from it that only this late alteration of affection created the American

---

[3] John Locke, *Two Treatises of Government*, ed. Peter Laslett (New York: New American Library, 1965), II, secs. 138, 140.

[4] Ibid., II, sec. 222.

[5] "Not only soldiers of our common blood, but Scotch and foreign mercenaries." Quotations from Jefferson's Declaration, as well as from the final version, are from *Portable Jefferson*, pp. 235–41. Garry Wills interpolates "British and American" into Jefferson's "our common blood." *Inventing America: Jefferson's Declaration of Independence* (Garden City, N.Y.: Doubleday, 1978), p. 311.

[6] Wills, *Inventing America*.

people or more generally that sentiment is what constitutes a people. Although Locke himself observed that "those, who liked one another so well as to joyn into Society, cannot but be supposed to have some Acquaintance and Friendship together, and some Trust one in another," he did so only to explain why early societies had failed to think of methods for restraining and balancing government.[7]

Whereas Congress renounced allegiance to the British crown and dissolved all political connection to "the State of Great Britain," Jefferson's draft not only renounced allegiance to the crown but dissolved all political connection "which may heretofore have subsisted between us and the people or parliament of Great Britain." But although Jefferson's version here again raises the question of peoples, he too writes only of "political connection" rather than allegiance, unity, or dependence, and his formulation leaves open whether and what political connection "may" have subsisted. Yet in his version's recounting of the American appeals to their British brethren, Jefferson makes tolerably clear that the only political connection was "one common king, . . . a foundation for perpetual league and amity," not political incorporation. Indeed Americans must already have been a distinct people to adopt the British king, to exercise the right of constituting their own forms of government. Most crucially, Jefferson's version of the past appeals includes the fact that Americans' "emigration and settlement here . . . were effected at the expense of our own blood and treasure." He had explained two years earlier, in "A Summary View of the Rights of British America," that Americans had already exercised the right of establishing independent new societies when they first exercised their natural right of emigration, when their country "had been acquired by the lives, the labors and the fortunes of individual adventurers."[8] The acts of naturally free individuals, in particular the expenditure of the life, labor, and property that by nature belong to each of them, are what constitute a people. The Declaration recapitulates and reconfirms that ultra-Lockean origin by its final pledge of signed individuals' lives, fortunes, and sacred honor.

Despite the Declaration's recounting of past appeals to the British on grounds of consanguinity, the people that is the locus of crucial political rights is not constituted by ethnicity or race. Indeed the Declaration complains that George was guilty of "obstructing the laws for naturalization of foreigners" and "refusing to pass others to encourage their migrations hither." It is true that the Declaration clearly does not consider a part of the American people the Indians

---

[7] Locke, *Two Treatises*, II sec. 107.

[8] *Portable Jefferson*, pp. 4–6.

whom George tried to use against them. And Jefferson's condemnation both of the slave trade and of the instigation of slave rebellion, omitted by Congress, clearly regards the slaves as "one people" distinct from the Americans as "another." But these distinctions are not based on race. The Indians in question live on or beyond our "frontiers" and according to the "rule of warfare" of "merciless . . . savages." Such uncivilized conduct is not a matter of race: George's own "cruelty and perfidy" are declared "scarcely paralleled in the most barbarous ages, and totally unworthy the head of a civilized nation." And the slaves are not even denominated by race or place of origin: they are called only "a distant people" carried into slavery "in another hemisphere" in violation of the "most sacred rights of life and liberty," which they possess by virtue of their "human nature." If these Indians are separated from the Americans by the crimes they commit, the slaves are separated by the crimes committed against them.

Even without Jefferson's explicit recognition of the human nature and sacred rights of the slaves, the Declaration is an emphatically universal rather than a racial or ethnic document, despite the animadversions of the Supreme Court in *Dred Scott* and of certain twentieth-century radicals. Its argument is founded on the rights of "all men"; the circumstances it describes are not unique but regular occurrences in the course of "human events"; the Americans have behaved in accordance with "all experience" of "mankind"; and it is addressed to "a candid world" from "a decent respect to the opinions of mankind."

Free individuals gave their lives, labor, and fortunes to constitute Americans a distinct people. What made them a distinct people was not their race or ethnicity but that they were (in another of Jefferson's phrases omitted by Congress) "a people fostered and fixed in principles of freedom," principles rooted in human nature and accessible to all mankind. The crucial political rights are exercised by distinct peoples but on behalf of the natural rights that belong to individuals and in accordance with principles that belong to all mankind.

Even Washington's apparently simple statement in his farewell address to his fellow citizens that "unity of government . . . constitutes you one people" rests on a more complex account of what constitutes the American people. He went on to derive their attachment to "the name of American" from facts that lay beneath unity of government and political independence:

> With slight shades of difference, you have the same religion, manners, habits, and political principles. You have in a common cause fought and triumphed together. The independ-

ence and liberty you possess are the work of joint councils
and joint efforts, of common dangers, sufferings, and suc-
cesses.

Addressing fellow "citizens by birth or choice of a common country,"
Washington explained peoplehood not by common descent or even
simply by unity of government, but by common mores and principles,
common deliberation, and common risk of life and property for
liberty.[9]

The question of peoplehood is not merely theoretical. If the
Americans were only a part of the British people, loyalists could defend parliamentary jurisdiction by using Lockean principles to argue
that when men "enter into Society to make one People, one Body
Politick under one Supreme Government," then "the *Majority* have
a Right to act and conclude the rest," and "there can be but *one
Supream Power,* which is *the Legislative.*"[10] Advocates of states'
rights would always have to contend with the Constitution's claim
that Americans constituted one people. That issue, or the question
whether a minority could exercise the rights that according to the
Declaration belong to a people, was tested by a great civil war. The
American people, in the words of Lincoln, rejected "the central idea
of secession" as "the essence of anarchy" and a principle of disinte-
gration "upon which no government can possibly endure."[11] Individuals may leave their old country and form a new people by making
settlements through their own blood, toil, and treasure; but a minority
may not divide a country at their own convenience and without meeting their obligations.

## Rights and Humanity

This conception of the rights of individuals and peoples that underlies
the American Constitution is clearly different from a conception of
political life as being directly devoted to the rights of humanity as a
whole. Individuals have a right to the pursuit of happiness; they are
not obligated to devote their lives to humanity. Individual rights
are properly secured by distinct peoples' instituting and altering their
own governments on such principles and in such forms as seem most
likely to them to effect their safety and happiness. These rights are

---

[9] "Farewell Address," in *A Compilation of the Messages and Papers of the
Presidents: 1789–1902,* ed. James D. Richardson (Washington: Bureau of National Literature and Art, 1907), vol. 1, p. 215.

[10] Locke, *Two Treatises,* II, secs. 89, 95, 149.

[11] Abraham Lincoln, *The Collected Works of Abraham Lincoln,* ed. Roy P.
Basler (New Brunswick, N.J.: Rutgers University Press, 1953), vol. 4, pp. 268, 436.

universal, but their security is primarily something each people must accomplish for itself. This is the result not of amoral relativism or selfish isolationism but of the very universal rights of individuals and peoples America is founded on. In Locke's political teaching, the natural duty of the individual to preserve all mankind as far as possible becomes particularized into the duty of civil society to preserve its own members.[12] Civil society has the right to secure the rights only of those who have consented to it. The enduring fame of Lafayette, Paine, Steuben, and Kosciusko testifies to the gratitude of the American people for the assistance provided during the Revolution by cosmopolitans ready to fight for human rights anywhere. But individual Americans are not famous for reciprocating by fighting in French, English, German, or Polish revolutions. With the first *Federalist*, we have believed that American patriotism is the most effective form of philanthropy, that making a success of our own political experiment is the greatest service we can perform for humanity.[13]

Although this conception of the rights of individuals and peoples differs from total and direct devotion to the rights of humanity as a whole, it does not imply indifference to the rights of foreign peoples and individuals. Henry Clay explained as clearly as any American statesman that "perhaps the care of the interests of one people is sufficient for all the wisdom of one legislature; and that it is among nations as among individuals that the happiness of the whole is best secured by each attending to its own peculiar interests."[14] When it came to the rights, rather than the interests, of others, however, Clay thought we could not remain indifferent. Expressing his sympathy for the South American revolution, he asked his fellow representatives rhetorically whether this republic, as practically "the sole depository of political and religious freedom," could "remain passive spectators of the struggle of those people to break the same chains which once bound us."[15]

Clay quoted Washington's expression of "sympathetic feelings . . . whensoever, in any country, I see an oppressed nation unfurl the banners of freedom" and warned that we would condemn our own founders and Revolution if we denied "that an oppressed people are authorized, whenever they can, to rise and to break their fetters." In

---

[12] Locke, *Two Treatises*, II, secs. 6–8, 11, 88, 128–29, 134–35, 159.

[13] *Federalist* No. 1, p. 33.

[14] "On American Industry," in *The Works of Henry Clay*, ed. Calvin Colton (New York: G. P. Putnam's Sons, 1904), vol. 6, p. 281.

[15] "On Sending a Minister to South America," in *Henry Clay*, vol. 6, p. 244; compare "Emancipation of the South American States," vol. 6, p. 146; "On the Greek Revolution," vol. 6, p. 249.

that same breath he declared, "I am no propagandist. I would not seek to force upon other nations our principles and our liberty, if they did not want them. I would not disturb the repose even of a detestable despotism." A people's exercise of its right to give or withhold consent made a crucial difference. He therefore added that "if an abused and oppressed people will their freedom; if they seek to establish it; if, in truth, they have established it; we have a right, as a sovereign power, to notice the fact, and to act as circumstances and our interest require."[16] As to what actions were so required, he had long declared that "it would undoubtedly be good policy to take part with the patriots of South America," that to do so was both our right and our interest, and that "the cause of humanity would be promoted by the interposition of any foreign power" that should end that "bloody and cruel war."[17]

The view of the rights of peoples derived from the Declaration and underlying the Constitution that led Clay to support other peoples' struggles for independence also led him to say that "the nature of their governments . . . is a question, however, for themselves. . . . We have no right to prescribe for them. They are, and ought to be, the sole judges for themselves." Yet he admitted he was "anxious . . . they should be free governments," imitating our example.[18] Indeed he proudly expressed the hope that "we should become the center of a system which would constitute the rallying-point of human freedom against all the despotism of the old world," a view "infinitely more gratifying" than the perspective of mere interest.[19] The rights of individuals and peoples dictate an attachment to human freedom but do not authorize any individual or people to exercise the rights of humanity.

## Rights and Nationality

The underlying American constitutional conception of the rights of individuals and peoples differs also from any view of politics that focuses on the rights of nations as such, or of peoples understood as nations. Our Constitution has inspired ardent patriotism and national pride, but its principles are incompatible with the modern nationalism that subordinates all else to the rights of an entity defined by land, blood, language, culture, custom, and history. Those bonds command

---

[16] "Emancipation of the South American States," p. 142.
[17] "On the Direct Tax," in *Henry Clay*, vol. 6, pp. 96–97.
[18] "Emancipation of the South American States," p. 145.
[19] "On Sending a Minister to South America," p. 243.

our respect, but they are not the source of rights. John Jay in *Federalist* No. 2 suggests that

> Providence has been pleased to give this one connected country to one united people—a people descended from the same ancestors, speaking the same language, professing the same religion, attached to the same principles of government, very similar in their manners and customs, and who, by their joint counsels, arms, and efforts, fighting side by side throughout a long and bloody war, have nobly established their general liberty and independence.[20]

But appeal to the notion that "it was the design of Providence that an inheritance so proper and convenient for a band of brethren, united to each other by the strongest ties, should never be split" promptly gives way to concentration on what makes national unity so convenient, what reasons support the people's "strong sense of the value and blessings of union."[21] *Federalist* No. 3 treats the American people's attachment to the Union as an "opinion respecting their interests."[22] Even the political existence of the nation must be justified by the advantages it offers the people, rather than by the ties of nationality.

Lincoln also argued for national unity from the unity of the land when he confronted attempted secession in his First Inaugural Address. He elaborated that argument in his annual message to Congress in 1862, in which he explained that "a nation may be said to consist of its territory, its people, and its laws," of which only the land is "ever-enduring." His consideration of that permanent constituent of the American nation revealed that "there is no line, straight or crooked, suitable for a national boundary, upon which to divide," that our land "demands union and abhors separation."[23] But almost as soon as he warned that "physically speaking, we cannot separate," he admitted that "this country, with its institutions, belongs to the people who inhabit it," who retain "their *revolutionary* right to dismember" it.[24] Unity of land, like that of blood, language, or culture, may be a powerful consideration for a people to weigh in exercising

---

[20] *Federalist* No. 2, p. 38.

[21] Ibid., pp. 38–39. Similarly, Washington's farewell address finds "the most commanding motives" for preserving the union not in the inducements of sympathy quoted earlier in this paper, but in considerations of interest. "Farewell Address," p. 215.

[22] *Federalist* No. 3, p. 42.

[23] *Lincoln*, vol. 5, pp. 527–29.

[24] Ibid., vol. 4, p. 269 (emphasis in original).

their right to constitute, preserve, or dismember a nation; but those authoritative political rights belong to peoples not constituted by nationality and may even be exercised at the expense of nationality. What made the Union sacred for Lincoln was not the unity of the land or nationality but its status as an experiment in self-government, designed to secure the rights of all.

Although *The Federalist* does not derive decisive political rights from nationality, it is emphatically nationalist in another sense: it argues that the people's safety and happiness can best be secured by instituting a strong federal government with the military, fiscal, and commercial powers necessary to conduct an energetic foreign policy and maintain an effective defense. It accepts Hobbes's answer to the question of how to secure rights as the beginning, though not the whole, of constitutional wisdom. Its distinctive argument for the advantages of national unity, however, is that a large republic is most able "to secure the public good and private rights" against the danger of faction.[25] In other words, the most famous American argument for our nationhood is so far from subordinating individuals to the rights of the nation that it judges even the existence of the nation at the bar of security for private rights.

*The Federalist*'s argument for national unity is far from nationalist reliance on tradition or history. It culminates in *Federalist* No. 14 with an appeal to "the people of America, knit together as they are by so many cords of affection," not to listen to "the unnatural voice" that advocates disunion or to let "a blind veneration for antiquity, for custom, or for names" prevent them from adding "the experiment of an extended republic" to "the numerous innovations displayed on the American theater in favor of private rights and public happiness," which included "a revolution which has no parallel in the annals of human society" and "governments which have no model on the face of the globe."[26] The familiar paradox of a tradition of innovation and revolution rules out not only a consistent American conservatism but also an American nationalism that derives rights from custom.

*Federalist* No. 14 also declares that "the kindred blood which flows in the veins of American citizens, the mingled blood which they have shed in defense of their sacred rights, consecrate their Union," but ultimately that is because what is sacred is their rights, not their blood.[27] *Federalist* No. 24 remarks that "politicians have ever with great reason considered the ties of blood as feeble and pre-

---

[25] *Federalist* No. 10, p. 80.
[26] *Federalist* No. 14, pp. 103–4.
[27] Ibid.

carious links of political connection."[28] Our Constitution secures rights that belong to American citizens as individuals and as a people constituted by consent and not by blood. It has nothing in common with today's terrorist organizations and international declarations that invoke "national rights" as bloody altars on which to sacrifice the rights of individuals and smother the voices of consent.

## Rights and Race

Closely related differences distinguish the rights secured by the American Constitution from rights of races or ethnic groups. The political arrangements of the Constitution excluded enslaved blacks and autonomous Indians, rather than blacks or Indians as such. The Constitution employed elaborate circumlocution to avoid the mention of slavery as well as race: slaves are described as "all other Persons" besides "free Persons" (Article I, section 2); "such Persons as any of the States now existing shall think proper to admit" (Article I, section 9); a "Person held to Service or Labour in one State, under the Laws thereof" (Article IV, section 2).[29] The word "slavery" first appears in the Constitution only with its prohibition in the Thirteenth Amendment.

*Federalist* No. 11 even argued that the Constitution would enable the United States to teach moderation to a Europe that had dominated Africa, Asia, and America and considered "the rest of mankind as created for her benefit." The United States could "vindicate the honor of the human race" and refute the "arrogant pretensions of the European" to "a physical superiority."[30]

The exclusion of slaves and "Indians untaxed" from the political arrangements of the original Constitution stemmed not from any explicitly racial character of the Constitution as an instrument of white rights but from the conjunction of implicit racial practices with explicit nonracial devotion to the property rights of individuals. Some Indians were excluded from taxation and representation as outside the economy of commercial property. Commerce with them could be included neither in that "with foreign Nations" nor in that "among

---

[28] *Federalist* No. 24, p. 161 (the remark is made in the context of dynastic connection).

[29] Lincoln explained that "the Framers of the Organic Law believed that the Constitution would *outlast* Slavery and they did not want a word there to tell future generations that Slavery had ever been legalized in America." *Lincoln,* vol. 3, p. 496.

[30] *Federalist* No. 11, pp. 90–91.

the several States" (Article I, section 8). Some blacks were excluded as slaves deprived of all property.

The implicit contradiction between the Constitution's accommodation to racist practices and its fundamental commitment to the rule of law and to the rights of individuals to life, liberty, and property was resolved only by later amendments; and its practical effects remain more than a century later. The Thirteenth Amendment explicitly affirmed the meaning of the rule of law already suggested by the separation of powers and the Fifth Amendment, that individuals can be deprived of liberty only "as a punishment for crime whereof the party shall have been duly convicted." The Fourteenth Amendment made clear that "all persons born or naturalized in the United States and subject to the jurisdiction thereof, are citizens of the United States and of the State wherein they reside" without singling out the blacks previously excluded by some states. It also extended the protection of due process and equal protection of the laws to all persons and against the states and first explicitly introduced "the right to vote" into the Constitution. Race first appeared explicitly in the Constitution only in the Fifteenth Amendment's provision that the right to vote shall not be abridged "on account of race, color, or previous condition of servitude." The amended Constitution protects the rights of individuals against violation on the basis of their race, not rights of racial or ethnic groups as units. It protects the rights of individuals not as members of racial or ethnic groups but despite their membership. The Civil War settled not only that Americans are one people whose rights cannot be exercised by states or minorities but that all Americans are part of that one people.

Neither locus of rights—the authoritative political whole, the people, or the fundamental political part, the individual—is defined by race. The rights of the people the Constitution expresses and secures have nothing in common with the racial rights, whether Aryan, Arab, Afrikaner, or African, that have animated certain other constitutions. Although, as we shall see, the Constitution's rights of the people imply rights for majorities and even a form of majority rule, the rightful majority is not racial or ethnic. The Constitution's conception of rights is equally opposed to black rule in Africa and to white rule in America. Whatever prudent policy may dictate in particular circumstances and whatever measures may be necessary to incorporate into one people those originally excluded as another, the Constitution was not intended to secure the rights of racial or ethnic groups to their own distinct political representation, for example, or to proportional percentages in prestigious professions or remunerative occupations. Such groups, of course, may have interests of their own, which some of their members may organize to promote politically, but they may not claim collective racial or ethnic rights to which others must accord constitutional respect.

## Rights and Class

The rights the Constitution secures are not those of socioeconomic classes as such, either. The prohibitions against granting titles of nobility manifest rejection of the conception of a constitution as a bulwark of the rights of an aristocracy. But the Constitution is also remote from such later conceptions as a Marxist dictatorship of the proletariat, a fascist or corporatist representation of classes, or a social democratic government conceived of as custodian of a social contract between classes.

*Federalist* No. 10 may remind us of views that attribute rights to classes. But it argues that an extensive modern republic, such as the Constitution was designed for, includes so many different interests that the governing majority could not be composed of any one class, but would be, in the words of *Federalist* No. 51, "a coalition of a majority," usually formed on principles of "justice and the general good."[31] Unlike Marxists, Madison regards the radical division between those who hold and those who are without property as characteristic not of modern society with its highly developed differentiation of "different degrees and kinds of property" but of ancient society.[32] Hamilton's *Federalist* No. 35 rejects "an actual representation of all classes of the people by persons of each class" as not only "altogether visionary" but also contrary to "any arrangement that leaves the votes of the people free." It rejects the claim that a representative belonging to one class cannot understand and attend to the "interests and feelings" of members of another. In particular, a member of "the learned professions" can serve well as "an impartial arbiter," making judgments "as it shall appear to him conducive to the general interests of the society." The essence of republican representation is not the representative's class membership but his dependence "on the suffrages of his fellow-citizens" and "the necessity of being bound, himself and his posterity, by the laws to which he gives his assent."[33] The rights of individuals to vote and to the rule of law,

---

[31] *Federalist* No. 51, p. 325.

[32] Compare ibid., No. 10, p. 78, and his speech of June 6, 1787, at the convention, in *The Mind of the Founder: Sources of the Political Thought of James Madison,* ed., Marvin Meyers (Indianapolis: Bobbs-Merrill, 1973), p. 102.

[33] *Federalist* No. 35, pp. 214–16; compare *Federalist* No. 57, pp. 351–53.

rather than the rights of classes as such, are what protect the interests of classes.

*Federalist* No. 10's argument is primarily about the interests rather than the rights of classes. Those interests are the byproducts of governmental protection of the different and unequal faculties of men, "from which the rights of property originate." The interests of classes derive from the more fundamental property rights of individuals. The overriding concern of *Federalist* No. 10 is to render those interests compatible with the rights of individuals and the public good of the whole people.[34] Madison's derivation of class interests from individual property rights was not merely theoretical; it was an expression of the fact that "in Governments like ours a constant rotation of property results from the free scope to industry, and from the laws of inheritance," so that there is not only a wide "actual distribution" but a "universal hope of acquiring property."[35]

Lincoln explained that ours is "that form, and substance of government, whose leading object is, to elevate the condition of men—to lift artificial weights from all shoulders—to clear the paths of laudable pursuit for all—to afford all, an unfettered start, and a fair chance, in the race of life."[36] He thought it "best for all to leave each man free to acquire property as fast as he can," although he also included "providing for the helpless young and afflicted" within "the legitimate object of government," which is "to do for the people what needs to be done, but which they can not, by individual effort, do at all, or do so well, for themselves."[37] Lincoln sided with the view that "labor is prior to, and independent of capital; that, in fact, capital is the fruit of labor, and could never have existed if labor had not *first* existed . . . that labor is the superior—greatly the superior—of capital."[38] That insight led Lincoln, not to a doctrine of class warfare, but to a recognition that there is no fundamental opposition between capital and labor in "free society." His defense of the right of laborers to strike was not fundamentally the affirmation of the right of one class against another but a defense of the right of the individual hired-laborer to "quit when he wants to," to "work for himself afterward, and finally to hire men to work for him." He could conclude that "while we do not propose any war upon capital, we do

---

[34] *Federalist* No. 10, pp. 77–84.

[35] Meyers, *Mind of the Founder*, pp. 439, 504.

[36] *Lincoln*, vol. 4, p. 438; compare p. 240.

[37] Ibid., p. 24; vol. 2, p. 221.

[38] Ibid., vol. 3, p. 478.

wish to allow the humblest man an equal chance to get rich with everybody else."[39]

## The Rights of Majorities and Minorities

Although the Constitution is fundamentally concerned with the rights of individuals and of the people rather than of such groups as races or classes, the security of individual and popular rights rests practically on the operation of majority and minority rights. These practically crucial group rights, however, are for the sake of the rights of their individual members or of the whole people and must be subordinate to them. Locke argued that "the *act of the Majority* passes for the act of the whole" so individuals can form a people that acts without requiring the "consent of every individual."[40] Any given majority has its rights not as a distinct unit but as a stand-in for the whole people, just as the rights of minorities are those of their individual members, not rights of the minority as a unit against its individual members. The Constitution's majority is not a fixed ruling part, like the *demos* in the classical conception of democracy. As Lincoln said, "A majority, held in restraint by constitutional checks, and limitations, and always changing easily, with deliberate changes of popular opinions and sentiments, is the only true sovereign of a free people."[41] Because the constitutional majority does not rule in its own right, it is properly neither a permanent and exclusive unit nor a momentary mob. Constitutional majority rule means, as *The Federalist* put it, that "the cool and deliberate sense of the community," not "every sudden breeze of passion" or "every transient impulse" or "momentary inclination," should "ultimately prevail."[42]

American constitutionalism is not populist majoritarianism, but neither is it a license for bureaucracies or courts to prevent deliberate popular control over government. The advantage of republican government is that the people are not compelled to resort to resistance to assert their control. Courts may have to protect individual rights even against bureaucracies and legislatures expressing popular impulses, but always at a cost in thwarted popular control and resulting popular alienation. The public character of public norms is most faithfully served when they are affirmed by the people through the political process. Judicial activism, like the executive veto or senatorial delib-

---

[39] Ibid., vol. 4, pp. 24–25.

[40] Locke, *Two Treatises*, II, secs. 96–98.

[41] *Lincoln*, vol. 4, p. 268.

[42] *Federalist* Nos. 63, 71, and 78, pp. 384, 432, 469.

eration, may give the people "time and opportunity for more cool and sedate reflection" until "ill humors . . . give place to better information, and more deliberate reflection" and "reason, justice, and truth can regain their authority over the public mind."[43] Settlement of cases one by one may direct public attention to structural defects that demand reform. Judicial review should always be a reluctant last resort, but judicial efforts at structural reform are especially at odds with popular rights insofar as such efforts are less episodic or exceptional and tend to make over or take over institutions that should be subject to popular control. If every institution goes into permanent receivership, popular rights are at an end. Populists and elitists may provoke and deserve each other, but neither should usurp the mantle of American constitutionalism.

## The Form of Our Rights and Alternatives to Rights

So far I have considered how the Constitution of the United States differs from alternative conceptions of constitutionalism by virtue of the possessors of the rights it secures. But the American conception of individual rights is distinguished not only by its locus but also by its form. The form of our rights is that they are primarily *rights to do, keep, or acquire things* and corresponding *rights not to have things done to us or taken from us.* This form contrasts, therefore, with alternative conceptions of *rights to have things done or given to one.* It presumes that individuals already have some of the essentials (such as life and liberty) and therefore need only to be secured in enjoying them and ordinarily have the ability to acquire other essentials (such as property, respect, truth, salvation) and therefore need only to be secured in pursuing them. Securing rights in this conception is a matter of providing security for enjoyment or pursuit, not of providing the desired objects of the rights themselves.

This formal difference is so close to the point of speaking about rights at all that its full bearing becomes apparent only through contrast with conceptions of constitutional goals that are best expressed without invoking rights. Some of these are closely allied, some merely compatible, some occasionally in tension, and others radically at odds with the American constitutional goal of securing rights.

Plato's *Republic* may offer us the deepest and widest understanding of the range of alternative conceptions of constitutional goals. The definition of justice that Socrates derives from Cephalus,

---

[43] *Federalist* Nos. 63 and 78, pp. 384, 469.

"the truth and giving back what a man has taken from another," agrees with the usage of Locke and *The Federalist* in identifying justice with respect for private property.[44] But Socrates' counter-example and Polemarchus' restatement, "that it is just to give to each what is owed," raise the more radical question of distribution, which leads eventually to communism (common ownership of property, spouses, and children) among the guardians.[45] The best regime of classical political philosophy is concerned not with the natural rights of individuals but with natural right, that which is right by nature. The American constitutional dedication to securing rights is not an answer to the question of distribution but the result of posing another question. If we cannot help asking what is owed to each and directing our political institutions to achieving the correct distribution, we shall be led far from the original conception of American constitutionalism. The most common answers today to the question of just distribution are, of course, far more egalitarian than Plato's.

As Plato proceeds to develop the best regime, however, just distribution becomes incidental to other goals. The diversity of those goals is most clearly shown by the diversity of the criteria Socrates invokes in demonstrating the goodness of the first two "waves," or characteristic features of his best regime, the equality of women and sexual communism. He argues for the first by asking, "Is there anything better for a city than the coming to be in it of the best possible women and men?"[46] He argues for the second by asking, "Have we any greater evil for a city than what splits it and makes it many instead of one? Or a greater good than what binds it together and makes it one?" (which he restates as "the community of pain and pleasure is the greatest good for a city").[47] The tension between the goals of the best possible human beings and the city "most like a single human being" is the great theme of the *Republic*.[48] What concerns us, however, is that from each of these comes a conception of politics distinct from securing rights.

Cultivating virtue, educating the best human beings, or producing doers of noble deeds, the salient formulations of the goal of the best regime for classical political philosophy generally, led away from

[44] Plato, *The Republic of Plato*, tr. Allan Bloom (New York: Basic Books, 1968), 331c. Compare Locke, *An Essay Concerning Human Understanding*, ed. Peter H. Nidditch (Oxford: Oxford University Press, 1975), IV, iii, 18, p. 549, and *Federalist* No. 10, pp. 77–81.

[45] Plato, *Republic*, 331e, 416d, 423e.

[46] Ibid., 456e.

[47] Ibid., 462ab, 464b.

[48] Ibid., 462c.

individual rights toward censorship, civic religion, and unlimited regulation and away from popular rights toward kingship and aristocracy. But concern for the development of human faculties as the highest political goal can also be found in Tocqueville's presentation of democracy in America. The "first object of government," according to *Federalist* No. 10, is the protection not of "the rights of property" as such but of "the faculties of men," from which those rights "originate."[49] The rights of popular participation or control as well as the individual rights of intellectual and economic self-reliance can be understood as the prerequisites for self-development.

The goal of unity, solidarity, community, or fraternity leads more unambiguously away from individual rights, but tends to reinforce the exercise of popular rights. In modern times this goal animates romantic movements of left and right more than liberal constitutionalism. But the longing for it has demanded some satisfaction even in a constitutional order where it is not the dominant goal. After all, the first goal avowed by the Constitution is "to form a more perfect Union." *The Federalist* indeed began its case for the Constitution by an argument for preserving national unity and expected the Constitution to contribute toward "a general assimilation" of the "manners and laws" of the states.[50] Yet our federal system has perhaps best provided for a sense of community on the local level. Precisely our respect for rights provides freedom to form congenial voluntary associations that nurture a more solid and less dangerous sense of fraternity than any modern mass state, however organized or animated, can offer. On the national level, Lincoln may have best articulated how our very shared commitment to the rights of the people and of the individual could also make us into a united moral community.

A Christian version of the political conception of unity or a community of pain and pleasure envisions a political order animated by love or charity. The modern liberal version speaks of compassion.[51] These versions tend to treat the liberalism of rights as a mean-spirited and pharisaical legalism. They are often more successful at letting the compassionate be generous with other people's money than at enabling the needy to do without compassion. They tend to be squeamish about inflicting the suffering needed to protect rights and oblivious of the suffering that compassionate acts themselves may

---

[49] *Federalist* No. 10, p. 78.
[50] *Federalist* No. 53, p. 334.
[51] For an incisive analysis of this phenomenon, see Clifford Orwin, "Compassion," *American Scholar*, vol. 49 (Summer 1980), pp. 309–33.

produce or perpetuate. Yet a cold constitutionalism of rights is continually driven to borrow human warmth from kinder sentiments.

Neither human virtue nor political unity precisely conveys the highest goal of Plato's best regime. The third "wave" Socrates introduces is, of course, the rule of philosopher-kings. His city is supposed to teach truth, or at least philosophy, the love of wisdom. Locke, in contrast, wrote that teaching the truth is no business of civil society.[52] The only means the Constitution expressly provides to "promote the Progress of Science" is "by securing for limited times to Authors and Inventors the exclusive Right to their respective Writings and Discoveries." Our government promotes truth by securing the rights of individuals that make its discovery more profitable and therefore more likely, by adding, as Lincoln said, "the fuel of *interest* to the *fire* of genius."[53]

Socrates understands the introduction to philosophy not as teaching true opinions but as conversion, as turning around the whole soul.[54] In the final myth of the *Republic*, he ties salvation of the soul in the afterlife to the practice of philosophy.[55] One can therefore plausibly say that there is a Christian version of the Platonic view of truth as the highest goal of the best regime, which regards salvation as the goal of politics. The First Amendment prohibition of a national establishment of religion prevents our government from trying to enforce or subsidize salvation; the protection of free exercise of religion prevents our government from interfering with the pursuit of salvation.

To compare the goals of the American Constitution with those of Plato's best regime, which "has its place in speeches," in heaven, or within the philosopher himself, is enlightening but neither just nor realistic.[56] It is more appropriate to compare the goals of the Constitution with those of the actual regimes with which Plato contrasts his best regime, the "bad" regimes, as he calls them.[57]

Before entering into specific comparisons with the particular regimes, we should contrast the very notion of *politeia* (translated regime or constitution) in classical political philosophy with the

---

[52] John Locke, *Epistola de Tolerantia/A Letter on Toleration*, ed. Raymond Klibansky and J. W. Gough (Oxford: Oxford University Press, 1968), pp. 122–23.

[53] *Lincoln*, vol. 3, p. 363.

[54] Plato, *Republic*, 518bc.

[55] Ibid., 619e.

[56] Ibid., 592ab; compare Polybius, *The Histories*, VI, 47, tr. W. R. Paton (London and Cambridge, Mass.: Loeb Classical Library, 1966), vol. 3.

[57] Plato, *Republic*, 445c, 449a; but compare 544a–545a.

American conception of a constitution. The *politeia* is the form taken by a political community, determined by who rules it. The dominant characteristic of the ruling part determines both the political goal of the whole regime and the personal goals of the individuals in it. This conception reflects the view that political rule is natural. The American conception of a constitution, in contrast, is that of a fundamental law, preferably written in a single document, understood as the expression of the will of the whole people. Whoever governs in accordance with it, therefore, acts not as the ruling part but as a representative of the whole people.[58] The Constitution grants powers to government from the natural rights of individuals, not so that some can rule others or form their goals, but so that the remaining rights of all can be more secure. If a constitution is a limiting grant of powers, the ancient regimes did not have constitutions with different goals; like modern totalitarian states, they did not really have constitutions at all.

The first of the actual regimes Plato presents he calls timocracy, the rule of honor.[59] Such rule by a warlike elite is dedicated to victory. The critique of this kind of regime, "the one that is praised by the many," occupies a special place in classical political philosophy.[60] Aristotle explains that "in most states, most of the laws are only a promiscuous heap of legislation; but we have to confess that where they are directed, in any degree, to a single object, that object is always conquest."[61] But even this regime is afflicted by mixed motives that render impossible an unequivocal statement of its goal.[62] Its dedication may be to the virtue of courage elicited by the struggle for victory, to the conquest, wealth, and enjoyment made possible by victory, or to the ambiguous goal of honor itself. Because it is at best devoted to only a part of virtue, it is at worst not devoted to virtue at all.[63]

While not every regime need seek conquest or pursue victory in itself, every regime must pursue victory in any contest that threatens its own freedom.[64] The preamble announces that the American Constitution is formed to "provide for the common defence" as one of its goals. *Federalist* No. 3 explained that "among the many objects to

---

[58] See *Federalist* No. 78, pp. 466–68.

[59] Plato, *Republic*, 544c–550b.

[60] Ibid., 544c; compare Plato, *Laws*, especially books 1 and 2, and Aristotle, *The Politics of Aristotle*, ed. Ernest Barker (Oxford: Oxford University Press, 1958), IV.i, sec. 6, and VII.xiv, secs. 16–17.

[61] Aristotle, *Politics*, VII.ii, sec. 9.

[62] Plato, *Republic*, 547b–548c.

[63] Aristotle, *Politics*, II.ix, secs. 34–35; VII.xv, sec. 6; VIII.iv, secs. 1–6.

[64] Ibid., VII.xiv, sec. 21.

which a wise and free people find it necessary to direct their attention, that of providing for their *safety* seems to be the first."[65] Securing rights means in the first place defending them. An eagerness to defend one's rights is still a far cry from a love of conquest. *Federalist* No. 8 explained another way that modern societies are different from "the ancient republics of Greece": "The industrious habits of the people of the present day, absorbed in the pursuits of gain and devoted to the improvements of agriculture and commerce, are incompatible with the condition of a nation of soldiers, which was the true condition of the people of those republics." Hamilton adds that, in a country like ours seldom exposed to invasions, the citizens are "not habituated to look up to the military power for protection" and "neither love nor fear the soldiery" but "view them with a spirit of jealous acquiescence in a necessary evil."[66] He even had to argue against the recurring American tendency to act as if "all that kind of policy by which nations anticipate distant danger and meet the gathering storm must be abstained from, as contrary to the genuine maxims of a free government."[67] Americans have often insisted on victory in war and have occasionally engaged in wars of conquest; but usually they have hoped to avoid even having to defend themselves.

*Federalist* No. 6 remarks that "Sparta was little better than a well-regulated camp; and Rome was never sated of carnage and conquest."[68] But ancient Sparta and Rome were by no means the last political communities directed toward military power or foreign conquest. Modern nationalist or ideological regimes, whether of the left or of the right, have marched in that same direction, though under newly inscribed banners. In contrast, the American dedication to the right of each people to institute or alter its own government justifies replacing the tyrannies of defeated aggressors with free constitutions, but it does not lend itself to wars of revolutionary conquest.

Plato presents oligarchy as the regime that honors wealth and is ruled by the wealthy.[69] Critics of the American Constitution have from the beginning criticized it as a disguised oligarchy.[70] Securing property rights is of special advantage not only to the wealthy but also to those who would acquire wealth. Public sanction for the free-

---

[65] *Federalist* No. 3, p. 42.

[66] *Federalist* No. 8, pp. 68–69.

[67] *Federalist* No. 25, pp. 165–66.

[68] *Federalist* No. 6, p. 57; compare Plato, *Laws*, 666e.

[69] Plato, *Republic*, 550c–555a.

[70] Compare *Federalist* No. 57, pp. 350–51.

dom to acquire wealth can degenerate into public worship of wealth, but it can also be kept free of such oligarchical perversion.

Plato presents democracy as the regime that defines freedom as the good and is ruled by the poor.[71] Americans often refer to the security of rights provided by the Constitution as freedom or liberty and call our political regime a democracy, but it differs radically from ancient democracy in both form and end. Neither the representatives who, in the American Constitution but not in ancient democracies, exclude *"the people in their collective capacity"* from any direct share in government nor "the great body of the people" from and by whom they are elected are defined as poor or rich.[72] Liberty articulated as rights is more specific and limited as well as more lawful than liberty understood as "license . . . to do whatever one wants."[73]

It is unnecessary to compare the American Constitution with tyranny, the worst of the actual regimes Plato discusses.[74] A society ruled by a constitution or fundamental law is far from lawless enslavement to an individual. But the Platonic account of the goal of tyranny presents the conception that has most succeeded in usurping the place of rights as a political goal in contemporary understanding. Plato's presentation of tyranny requires a psychological restatement of the goals of oligarchy and democracy. Oligarchy satisfies only the "necessary desires" that "conduce to money-making" and enslaves "the other desires" that are "spendthrifty" and "are called unnecessary," whereas democracy establishes "equality" between the necessary and unnecessary desires.[75] Plato distinguishes further among the unnecessary desires between those that "are hostile to law" and innocent ones that perhaps "exist for the sake of play." Tyranny is the rule of the "terrible, savage, and lawless form of desires" that exists in every man but is usually repressed, revealed only in dreams of intercourse "with a mother or with anyone else at all—human beings, gods, and beasts"—of foul murder, or of forbidden food.[76]

This psychological level of the Platonic diagnosis of actual political regimes presents us with a familiar political goal: the satisfaction of desire. Its modern versions from Machiavellianism through utility and the greatest good of the greatest number to interest-group bargaining and preference curves have all too often displaced rights in

---

[71] Plato, *Republic*, 555b–562c.

[72] *Federalist* No. 63, pp. 386–87; No. 39, p. 241; No. 57, p. 351.

[73] Plato, *Republic*, 557b; compare Locke, *Two Treatises*, II, secs. 22, 57.

[74] Plato, *Republic*, 564a–576b.

[75] Ibid., 554a, 558d–559d, 561bc, 572c.

[76] Ibid., 571b–575a. Compare 581e.

our political discourse. Machiavelli's prince and Plato's tyrant remind us that the general conception of the satisfaction of desire as a goal leaves unanswered the crucial personal and political questions whether all desires are equal, whether some must be repressed, and whether some must reign over the rest. At the same time, as we retreat from moral and political nightmares toward the security of rights, we may admit that the question of the satisfaction of desire cannot be avoided. Our Constitution secures the rights of individuals to seek satisfaction for their desires, but it is compelled to distinguish lawful from lawless desires. Exclusive reliance on rights generates irritable litigiousness and empty yearning. Our public discourse is impoverished if we only invoke our rights and never debate what is good for us, if we only assert our right to pursue happiness and never discuss what would make us happy.

## Conclusion

The preamble to the Constitution reminds us that our conception of the goals of the Constitution is not exhausted by rights or liberty. *The Federalist* pairs private rights with the public good. The highest and hardest task of American statesmen and citizens is to weigh our fundamental commitment to individual and popular rights against the sometimes competing claims of the cause of humanity, the sentiments of nationality, the prejudices of race, the interests of class, the demands of justice, the cultivation of virtue, the striving for community, the impulse of compassion, the higher callings of truth and salvation, the allure of prosperity, and the necessity of defense.

A NOTE ON THE BOOK

*This book was edited by*
*Gertrude Kaplan and Ellen Dykes,*
*of the AEI Publications staff.*
*Pat Taylor designed the cover and format.*
*The text was set in Palatino, a typeface designed by Hermann Zapf.*
*Maryland Linotype, of Baltimore, Maryland, set the type,*
*and R. R. Donnelley & Sons Company,*
*of Harrisonburg, Virginia, printed and bound the book,*
*using permanent, acid-free paper made by the S. D. Warren Company.*

## DATE DUE

| | | | |
|---|---|---|---|
| ~~NOV 3 0 '92~~ | | | |
| il! 4630414 sent 11-15-91 | | | |
| | | | |
| | | | |
| | | | |
| | | | |
| | | | |
| | | | |
| | | | |
| | | | |
| | | | |
| | | | |
| | | | |

DEMCO 38-297